Pimlico:
Deep Well of Glee

by Adam Stout

Westminster City Archives

To my parents, of course

ISBN 1 900893 01 0

WESTMINSTER
LIBRARIES
& ARCHIVES

Contents

Foreword

Growing up in Pimlico, Adam Stout has had a lifelong interest in its history. His use of the archives began as a schoolboy in short trousers, which accounts for his substantial, in-depth knowledge, not just of Pimlico's history, but of the sources from which this material can be gleaned. Over the years he has become familiar with the wealth of original documents and printed local history material held by Westminster City Archives, and his thorough approach to research has involved exploiting to the full the many different aspects of this unique collection.

Since 1995, material relating to the history of Westminster, Marylebone and Paddington has been brought together in a purpose-built City of Westminster Archives Centre. The vast collection of printed and documentary sources includes a copy of every important book on London, and some 60,000 photographs, prints, watercolours and drawings - a uniquely valuable record of the buildings and people of Westminster from 1650 to the present day. The earliest original document dates from 1256, and there is a particularly fine collection of maps and plans. A special theatre collection covers all West End theatres from the 18th century onwards.

The Archives Centre exists for the benefit of all those, now and in the future, with an interest in Westminster's fascinating past. Its aim is not only to preserve the local documentary heritage - the raw material for historical research - but also to raise awareness and promote access to this treasure-store, in particular through talks, exhibitions, contact with schools, and publications.

We hope that in publishing this book, Adam Stout's account of Pimlico's history will receive the wide audience which it deserves, and inspire others to dig deeper into the history of their local area. I am sure that readers will find *Pimlico: Deep Well of Glee* entertaining as well as informative, and full of intriguing detail.

Jerome Farrell
City Archivist

Westminster City Archives
10 St Ann's Street
London SW1P 2XR
(Tel: 0171 641 5180)

Introduction and Acknowledgements

I grew up in Pimlico during the 1960s and early 1970s, and it's a strange jumble of memories that I have of the place. The rattle of harness and clipping of hooves as the soldiers exercised their horses early in the morning; the low and mournful hoots of the barges as they took the city rubbish down the Thames at night; the *Morning Star* vendor doing the rounds of the back-streets; the Churton Street delicatessen with the glass-topped biscuit-bins cunningly placed at child-level; Frank Wright's cheerful grocer's shop in Cambridge Street; Sonny Bussey's greengrocery next door, cavernous and friendly; the BOAC Tower, Time itself, the neon letters glowing otherworld blue at night; a derelict, frightening house in Hugh Street, daylight shining through blackened rafters, gaping windows to the street; a mysterious green-barred gate on Ebury Bridge down to the end of a Victoria platform, always locked; the strange round rooftop reservoirs of Churchill Gardens. I left home in '75, and this seems like a good date at which to end this book. It also spares me - and you - from having to try and pretend objectivity about events that are too recent to feel dispassionate about.

Thanks are due to Edward Lloyd, and his now-defunct firm Marriotts, for financing my initial research, and to the Grosvenor Estate for allowing me the run of their archives, of which I have made but scant use for this book. But my biggest debt of thanks by far goes to the staff at Westminster City Archives - John, Roy, Alison, Elizabeth: old friends now, helpful, patient and inspiring as well; and to a new face there, Jill Barber, for her enthusiastic support of this venture.

Pimlico, like most London districts, has hazy and rather personal boundaries. My Pimlico runs from Vauxhall Bridge Road to Chelsea Bridge Road, from the river to the canal and railway. Some street names have changed: I always use the modern form, except where quoting, but some names to note are Willow Walk, rebuilt by Cubitt as Warwick Street, which in 1938 became Warwick Way; St George's Road, which became St George's Drive in 1940; and Stanley Street (Alderney Street in 1879). The rivers Tyburn and Westbourne are generally referred to in later records as the 'King's Scholars' Pond Sewer' and the 'Ranelagh Sewer' respectively: but I have used the older names, or sometimes both.

Most of the illustrations have been taken from the collections at Westminster City Archives. I am grateful for permission to publish the illustrations on the following pages: 12, 17 (top), 43,44 by permission of the British Library; 8, 75 (bottom) by permission of the Grosvenor Estate; 60 by permission of the London News Group; 30 (top), 34 (top) by permission of the Museum of London; 33 (top) by courtesy of the National Portrait Gallery, London; 67 copyright Rochester Press Limited; 11 copyright the Royal Collection Her Majesty the Queen; 73 by permission of UGC UK Limited; 9 by permission of the Dean and Chapter of Westminster.

Cover Illustration: The Monster tavern, watercolour by Thomas Hosmer Shepherd, 1857

1 A Waistcoat Edition of Holland

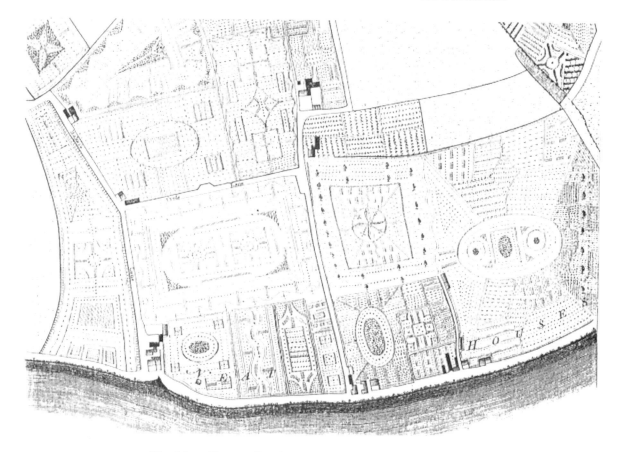

The Neat House Gardens on Horwood's map of 1795

Between Two Rivers

'Southward of the old King's Road has for 200 years been known as Pimlico', claimed R G Davis in 1859, but early writers were very vague about this sparsely-populated area on the edge of town. What we now consider 'Pimlico' was most commonly called the Neat Houses, or Neat House Gardens; the riverside was Millbank, later, more specifically, Thames Bank. Sometimes they ascribed this patch to Chelsea, sometimes to Tothill Fields, or Tothill-side. People may have been uncertain about what to call it, but the area has always been well defined, to east and west at least, by two little rivers. The Tyburn and the Westbourne both rise in North London, near Hampstead, and although they have both long since been encased and buried, their course is not hard to follow.

The Westbourne, first mentioned in the thirteenth century, after passing through Paddington (where Westbourne Terrace is one of several reminders), emerges in Kensington Gardens as the Serpentine. Today encased as the Ranelagh sewer, the river continues southwards beneath Knightsbridge and behind Lowndes Square. 'Bloody Bridge' carried the King's Road over the Westbourne: this area became known as the 'Five Fields', a desolate spot renowned for footpads, robbers and murderers, and this is doubtless how the bridge came by its name. A huge metal pipe today takes the river across Sloane Square station. It next runs under Holbein Place (in the nineteenth century delicately known as 'The Ditch'), crosses Pimlico Road, and weaves around the eastern edge of Chelsea Barracks to a point just above Chelsea Bridge. The Victorian arched entrance to the sewer is still there in the riverbank: the curious can walk into it at low tide.

The ornamental lake in Regent's Park is fed by the Tyburn, which gave its name to the

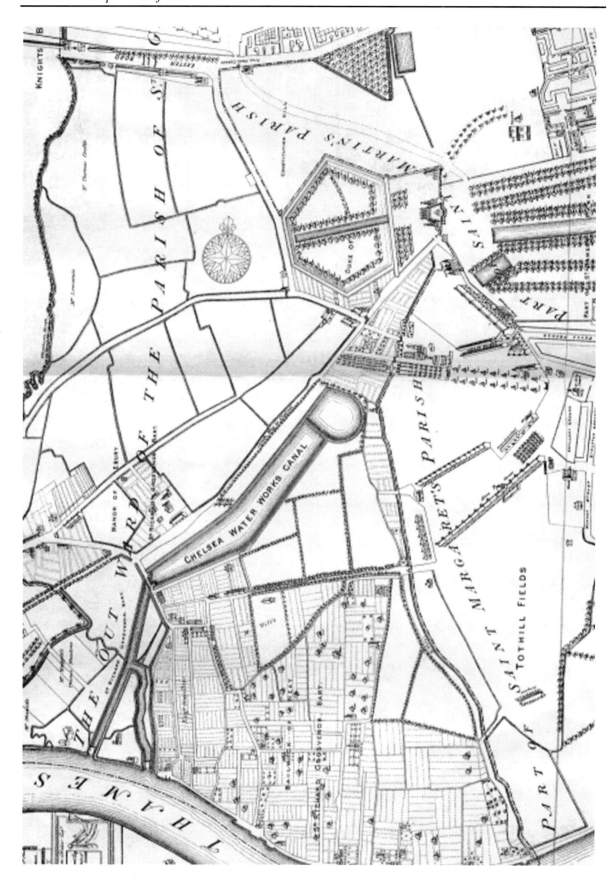

The Westbourne and the Tyburn defined the boundaries of the 'out ward' of St George, Hanover Square. The parish was created in 1725, when this map was produced.

The mouth of the Tyburn in 1808, when Westminster Abbey dominated the skyline.

infamous gallows near Marble Arch. A line of mist is said to mark the river's course beneath Green Park and the grounds of Buckingham Palace. The river then splits to form an island - the Isle of Thorney, on which Westminster Abbey and Palace came to be built. The western arm crosses beneath Stag Place and King's Scholars' Passage (in its later years, the river was known as the King's Scholars' Pond Sewer, the scholars in question being the pupils of Westminster School). Tachbrook Street (confusingly named after a village in Warwickshire) follows the Tyburn's windings through Pimlico to the Thames. This little river must have been pure enough in its day. Stag Brewery beers were made with Tyburn water, for the river ran through it; and in the thirteenth century pipes were built to carry its water to various conduits (Lamb's Conduit Street recalls one of them) nearer the city. But the Tyburn, like the Thames, became more and more polluted as the city expanded, and the royal family, which had been so pleased to acquire Buckingham Palace in 1762, found themselves with an unpleasant problem literally on their doorstep.

A solution was found in the building of a sluice-gate at the mouth of the river, which was closed at high tide to stop the Thames from sending its offerings to the Palace. The gate-keeper's house, now called 'Rio Cottage', still stands on Grosvenor Road, next to the modern Crown Reach flats; but the privilege of living on the job must have been pretty dubious. As late as 1857, people were complaining about the 'intolerable stench' at the confluence. Although the river itself now runs underground, a stretch of the eighteenth-century storm relief sewer nearly 700 feet long, and up to 35 feet wide, survived on the Tachbrook Estate until 1971: it was used in summer for cricket practice.

The two rivers served as parish, ward, city and parliamentary boundaries for centuries. The very name 'Tyburn' is derived from an old Frisian word meaning 'boundary stream', and a charter of 785 confirms that the river was then the boundary of Westminster. The area between the two rivers became the manor of Eia, which from the twelfth century was the personal fief of the Abbots of Westminster. When the abbey was dissolved

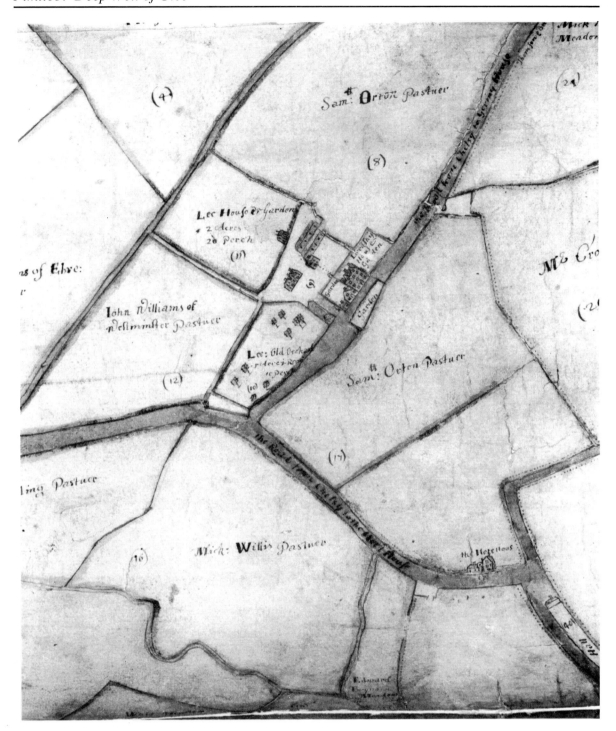

The Neat House and Ebury House ('Lordshipp House') from an estate map of 1675.

by Henry VIII, Eia became the 'Out Ward' of the parish of St Martin, and later still, of St George Hanover Square. A parish boundary stone can still be seen in the wall of a shop on the corner of Tachbrook Street and Warwick Way, which crossed the river via the Abbot's Bridge - a name still in use in the 1800s.

The Abbey and the Neyte

Imagine yourself to be standing on the Pimlico side of Ebury Bridge, with your back against the railway parapet, its brickwork still grimed by a century's worth of steam trains. You're looking down the length of Warwick Way, with Ebury Bridge itself to the left of you and Sutherland Street to the right, Churchill Gardens in the distance, and the blocks of the Abbot's Manor estate across the wide stretch of road in front of you. It's a blowy spot, but it's the highest piece of land in Pimlico today, and the great open tract of railway

line makes this a good place to get some feel for the place before it was developed. The railway line itself may be at about the original ground level, for Pimlico before development was low-lying, flood-prone and marshy - 'a stretch of fields with the usual allowance of ditches, rank grass, weeds, little pools of water, rushes and damp'. Massive infilling was needed before building could begin.

Looking from the same spot in 1550, you would notice a raised causeway following the route of Warwick Way across the meadows. It runs straight to Westminster Abbey a mile distant, and was presumably built by the abbots: the 'cawsey' is mentioned in 1536. The Abbey is easily the largest building on the skyline, although without its twin towers of course: they were not built until 1745. The track continues left over Ebury Bridge to a distant Chelsea, but the building you would have noticed most immediately lay just in front of you. This was the Neyte, the Abbot's Manor, built on a gravel spur that would probably appear as a slight hill. To the left is Ebury, once the main settlement here but during the Abbey's time probably the site of the Abbey farm.

The manor of Eye, or Eia, from which the name Ebury comes, was given to the Abbey of Westminster soon after the Norman Conquest. The Neyte itself, together with a mill, was purchased by the Abbey in 1235/6. Some suggest that the name is derived from 'neat', meaning 'cattle', and it is true that much of the land was used for pasture. The spelling of the name, however, suggests that the word 'neyte', like the 'eye' of Eia and Ebury, comes from 'eyot', meaning 'island', for the little hill that Neyte and Ebury were on was indeed an island in the flood-plain. The Abbot of Westminster was a powerful man, and his manor of the Neyte was a sumptuous residence. Fit for a king, indeed, for it was leased to Edward II for eleven years (1316 to 1327), when the facilities included a hall, pantry, buttery and garden. The Neyte was moated: a wise precaution, which may have spared the manor from destruction

during the Peasants' Revolt in 1381, when the rebels were burning property at Ebury, Tothill and Knightsbridge. John of Gaunt was less fortunate: his palace of the Savoy was sacked, and eight years later he was 'still without a place to suit us and our household'. The Abbot lent him Neyte, clearly still a suitable abode for the mighty.

Somewhere in the marshes hereabouts lived Margerie Gourdemaine, the Witch of Eye, burnt at Smithfield in 1441 because her 'sorcerie and witchcraft Dame Eleanor Cobham had long time used, and by her medecines and drinkes inforced the Duke of Gloucester to love hir ... after to wed hir'. Her spells did Dame Eleanor little good: two years later she was banished - after a three-day detention at the Neyte, from where she may well have been able to see the abode of the unfortunate Margerie.

Abbot John Islip died at the Neyte in 1532, and his funeral was an impressive affair. His body was accompanied on its last journey from the Neyte to the Abbey by so many mourners 'that the train was from Neyt until

Death of Abbot Islip at the Neyte.

The Neat House gardens in the early 19th century: note the horse-pump and flood barrier.

Tottel streete': the full length of the Causeway, including all of modern Warwick Way and Rochester Row. This display of pomp and power was perhaps a bit ill-timed. Four years later, the covetous Henry VIII took possession of Neyte and Ebury for himself.

The Neat House Gardens

The fertility of the Westminster flood-plain was proverbial. Labourers would 'refuse a pallace to droyle in these golden puddles', wrote John Norden in 1593:

The deepe and dirtie, loathsome soyle
Yields golden gaine to painful toyle.

Their right to 'droyle' was seriously restricted once Henry VIII had taken over, for the courtiers to whom he granted the land promptly enclosed the fields. It was a major blow to the parishioners of St Martin's. 'All the feldes .... that now be torned into meadow and pasture were arrable groundes and ancyent men saye that ther have byn 6 plowes more than now ys, to the Decay of husbandry'. In vain they requested 'that all the dyches wythe in every comon feald and the

hedges myght be cast down playne'. The land at 'the Net', as they lamented, was let out 'to them that will geve most mony for every acre', and against the power of the purse, the commoners stood little chance. In August 1592, a party of angry parishioners, led by the Bailiff of Westminster, marched to Ebury and tore down all the fences, but the enclosures continued.

The lands of the Neyte were particularly prized. Within a generation, the 'Neat House Gardens' became one of London's most famous market-gardens. As early as 1327, herbs and vegetables were being grown at the Neyte - lettuce, 'saveye' (Savoy cabbage?), borage and 'chirvill'. A seventeen-acre field just south of the Neat House was in 1614 called 'the gardens', but the Neat House Gardens were a product of the seventeenth century, and the rapid expansion of London and its hungry population. The Gardens soon acquired an excellent reputation. A play of 1632 extols 'the Neat House for musk-mellons and the gardens where we traffic for asparagus', and by 1675 there were well over twenty houses and cottages, most of them strung out along a lane that ran

south from the Neat House to the river, and along the riverbank itself.

These were the Neat Houses (note the plural), where Pepys and other Londoners were beginning to venture in pursuit of wine and recreation, and to see the gardens too, which suggests that some gardeners were growing ornamental plants and flowers. In May 1668, Pepys took a party of friends by water 'to one of the Neat Houses, where they walked in the gardens, but nothing but a bottle of wine to be had, they, though pleased with seeing the garden, went to Vauxhall'. A network of ditches was dug to drain and irrigate the ground. Dykes were built to protect the land from the regular Thames floodwaters - 'green sloping banks, gay with wild flowers during June', as a nineteenth-century resident recalled. The whole area, in the words of another, was like 'a waistcoat edition of Holland'.

By 1706, the Neat House Gardens were said to 'exceed all the other gardens in Europe for wholesome Produce and variety of Herbs ... [They] abound in Salads, early Cucumbers, Colliflowers, Melons, Winter Asparagus and almost every Herb fitting the Table'. Plenty of dung, and a market on their doorstep, were the reasons John Strype gave in 1720 for the gardeners' success: 'keeping the ground so rich by dunging it (and through the nearness of London they have the soil cheap) doth make the crops very forward, to their great profit in coming to such good markets'. Nearly a century later, one gardener claimed to be spreading 600 loads of dung each year on his nine acres.

The most famous of the Neat House Gardeners was Henry Wise, the 'Royal Gardener',

Henry Wise, the Royal Gardener.

who laid out grounds and gardens for successive monarchs and courtiers. Wise and his partner George London owned London's largest nursery at Brompton, and in 1712 were hailed by Addison as 'the heroic poets' of gardening. A year later, Wise acquired about twenty-four acres of land at the Neat House Gardens, which, like the gardens at Brompton, he may have used to cultivate fine and rare plants for the gardens of the wealthy. Wise died in 1738, but his Neat House lands remained in the hands of his descendants until well into this century. A pub in Warwick Way was named 'The Royal Gardener' in his honour - and kept that name until the 1980s, when, to the horror of gardeners everywhere, it became 'the Slug and Lettuce'.

2 Deepe Pimlyco, the Well of Glee

Elinour Rummin, purveyor of Pimlico.

Old Pimlico

Pimlico is a place that has moved with the times - about a mile in fact, for the original 'Pimplico' was a field opposite the modern Buckingham Palace, just south of the modern Stag Place. There is a reference from 1655 in the Grosvenor Estate archives to 'houses called Pimlico', which by the late eighteenth century was understood to refer to a muddle of mean streets on the site of Victoria Square. In 1816 Pimlico was quaintly described as 'a village or hamlet', and a year later as a street containing 48 houses. Old Pimlico was demolished in 1840, but Buckingham Palace itself was still considered to be in Pimlico as late as 1885.

By the 1820s at least, the name 'Pimlico' had come to include the area between the new

Grosvenor Canal (now the railway) and Ebury Street. Firms taking wharf space along the canal began to use 'Pimlico' in their names - the Pimlico Patent Bread Works, for instance, and the Pimlico Wheel Works. Modern Pimlico acquired the name almost as soon as building work began. In 1825, the canal was said to be '*at* Pimlico'; three years later, the new Eccleston Bridge, which linked Cubitt's new town with Belgravia and the north, was said to lead '*to* Pimlico'. Although Thomas Cubitt himself preferred the name 'South Belgravia', in the eyes of the Grosvenor Estate, the canal itself was always intended as a boundary between two distinct developments; and it seems that the growing self-definition of the grander scheme as 'Belgravia' left 'Pimlico' to serve as a name for all the rest.

It's a strange name, Pimlico. Place-name scholars, perhaps wisely, refuse to speculate on its origins or its meaning. But it is curious that this Spanish-sounding word first occurs in English at a time (1598) when, in spite of a certain antipathy to the Spanish in the wake of the Armada, a lot of Spanish words were entering the language: *cargo, cask, comrade, renegade, bravado*, for example. Various Native American words - *chocolate, avocado* - also came into English via Spanish at this date. There are several such names that sound a bit like 'Pimlico' - an extinct tribe, a bird, some very small islands - which has led some to speculate that our Pimlico might somehow be related. But if a Spanish origin is sought, then I'd plump for '*pimplar*', which means 'to booze', 'to tipple', 'to drink to excess'; and 'Pimlico' (or Pimplico, or Pimblico, as it was also spelt) as the place where the drinking was done. For this is the context in which 'Pimlico' first appears: as the name of an ale, and the ale-house that sold it.

In 1598 apparently, a satirical pamphlet appeared called *Newes from Hogsdon*, extolling the virtues of old Ben Pimlico and his nut-brown ale, brewed at Hoxton, near Shoreditch. Old Ben has acquired a legendary reputation, but he is only known from this one pamphlet - and the only known copy of *Newes from Hogsdon* has long since disappeared. The Hoxton tipple was certainly called Pimlico, whether or not Ben had once been brewing it. In 1609, the brewer was one Elinour Rummin, who became a legend in her own right: 'the famous Ale-wife of England', she was called in 1624. Pimlico ale was a brew of quite remarkable potency:

Back at least three yardes he reeles
'Pimlyco trips up good men's heeles'
(Lisping) he cryes, and downe he falls
Yet for more PIMLYCO still he calls.

Pimlico was the talk of the town for a generation. Between 1609 and 1616, it crops up no fewer than seven times in plays and pamphlets, always as a by-word for serious drinking. The craze reached its height in 1609: that April, two pamphlets in praise of Pimlico appeared within a fortnight. One of these has survived. 'Pimlyco, or runne Red-cap', which advises readers to 'bath your Braynes in Pimlyco', was clearly penned by an afficionado:

Of Pimlyco now let us sing,
Rich Pimlyco, the new-found Spring
Where men and women both together,
To warme their vaines in frosty weather,
Where men and women hot bloods coole,
By drincking Pimlycoes boyled poole
Strong Pimlyco, the nourishing foode
To make men fat, and breed pure blood;
Deepe Pimlyco, the Well of Glee,
That drawes up merry company.

Mistress Rummin's establishment at Hoxton spawned many imitations. A whole crop of 'Pimlicos' - most, if not all, presumably places of beer-blurred entertainment - sprang up across the country. A Pimlico-house in Oxfordshire is mentioned in 1642; another in Dublin in 1663; a Pimlico-house near Barnet and a Pimlico Gardens in Southwark (both in 1673); several others crop up during the eighteenth century.

The Westminster Pimlico was one of the first. The name is first found in 1625, and a decade later William Greene opened the Stag Brewery here, which can hardly be a coincidence. (The brewery flourished, and eventually became the headquarters of the Watney's empire until its demolition in 1959: Stag Place is on the site.) Although in 1780 it was said that the Westminster Pimlico had enjoyed the same reputation as its Hoxton counterpart, there are tantalisingly few references to it. Three pubs at least were to be found at Old Pimlico in the eighteenth century: the Elephant, the Fun, 'celebrated for its ales'; and the Bag O' Nails (probably a corruption of 'baccanales', meaning 'drunken revelry'), which, though rebuilt, still stands.

The Stag Brewery in 1817.

Demolishing Custards

The reputation of Pimlico expanded during the 1630s to include the excessive eating of cakes, puddings and custard-pies. A 'gentleman of valour' in Jasper Mayne's *The Citye Match* (1639) was said 'to squire his sisters and demolish custards at Pimlico'. Was he demolishing in Hoxton, or in Westminster? And might there be a connection with the famous Chelsea Bun House, later considered to be in Pimlico? For by now, the whole area between old Westminster and Chelsea was beginning to sprout pubs, pleasure-gardens, taverns, resorts and places of sometimes quite bizarre amusement to tempt the taste-buds of the city.

The Neat House gardens were already attracting Londoners in Pepys' day. In 1667 the tactless diarist took his wife and Mistress Knipp to the Gardens by coach, 'and there in a box in a tree they sat, and sang, and talked, and eat', though his wife was 'out of humour, as she always is when this woman is by'. It is tempting to think that this might have been the 'old tree, with table and seats for three in its branches' that survived until Vauxhall Bridge was built.

When Pepys visited the Neat Houses, he had to be content with a bottle of wine. Later tipplers were much better served. On the riverbank, by the Tyburn confluence, stood 'an old brick house called the Swan ale-house'; nearby stood the Naked Boy. The Plume of Feathers, in the Willow Walk (now Warwick Way), was gutted in 1766 by a fire which 'raged so fiercely that the family lost every thing; and the landlord was obliged to carry his wife (whom he had lately married) on his back, into the marshy ground behind the house, as it was impracticable to get through the flames in the front'. Fire was an

The wooden bridge in 1752.

occupational hazard for local publicans, it seems. The King's Arms, at the western end of the Willow Walk, was the resort of 'a friendly knot of gentlemen' who founded a Bowling Green Society there in 1755. This particular establishment very nearly disappeared when the landlord inadvertently ignited a hundred-gallon barrel of rum with a candle.

In 1723 the Chelsea Waterworks Company began to dig out the course of the modern railway for their reservoirs. This large, placid expanse of water became one of the area's attractions: 'on each side ... are handsome gravel walks, lighted with lamps and shaded with trees and hedges', wrote one admirer in 1762. A wooden bridge was built where Ebury Bridge now stands, to carry the old track from Chelsea to the Neat House and the ancient abbey causeway, now known as the Willow Walk. Wheeled traffic that might have been tempted to use the Walk as a short-cut to the city, avoiding the turnpike toll, found the way blocked at either end by great 'barricadoes' made from tree-trunks; but for pedestrians out from Westminster,

the Walk, with its avenue of pollarded willows, must then have been a pleasant one.

Near the bridge stood Jenny's Whim - a curious and highly popular institution, apparently established by a 'celebrated pyrotechnic' in the reign of George I. The 'Whim' was a substantial building, of red-brick and lattice-work, and part of it survived until the railway was widened in 1865. The grounds included a bowling-green, a fish-pond, a cock-pit and a pool where customers could enjoy 'the royal diversion of duck-hunting, with a decanter of Dorchester ale for sixpence'. The garden was dotted with arbours and recesses into which the unwary would venture; 'and treading on a spring, taking you by surprise, up started different figures, some ugly enough to frighten you, like a Harlequin, Mother Shipton, or some terrific animal'. Jenny's Whim attracted many wealthy patrons. It was a favourite place for city idlers, its rooms 'filled with talk and smoke', as a visitor observed disapprovingly. Here in 1755, in true Trivial Pursuit tradition, a group of tipplers compiled an impressive list of London notables which they called

Jenny's Whim: or a Sure Guide to the Nobility and Gentry - most of whom, the pamphlet implied, were regulars at the Whim. It seems probable that 'Jenny's Whim' was one and the same as the pub known as the Monster, which a sale advertisement of 1727 describes as 'a well-accustomed publick-house, together with some tenements and a large garden'. The pub was built on the site of the Neyte, sometime after the abbot had been forced to part with it. Another building, called the Neat House, was erected in its place: a simple picture on a map of 1675 suggests a two-storey building that may have become the pub. At one time, people thought that the name 'Monster' was a corruption of 'monastery': in 1887 it was said to have been the site of the old monastery garden - 'and had on one side the remains of its ancient wall'. More recent writers feel that the name is more likely to derive from some curiosity laid on to attract the customers, of the kind ascribed to Jenny's Whim, but it's always possible that the name recalls some legendary Grendel of the Pimlico marshes. 'Human bones have been found near the Monster', a lecturer of 1857 told an audience at the Pimlico Literary Institute, but maybe he was just trying to keep their attention. The Monster was rebuilt in 1856-58; the Pimlico bus used to terminate here, and the name, like the Elephant & Castle or the Angel, became familiar to people from all over London.

JENNY's WHIM;

OR A

SURE GUIDE

TO THE

Nobility, Gentry, and other Eminent Perfons, in this Metropolis ;

BEING A

GENUINE ACCOUNT

OF THEIR

TOWN-RESIDENCE,

Very different from the Romantic Pocket-Companions, Court and City Calendars, &c.

Books that only ferve to lead Strangers aftray.

Beware of Counterfeits, for fuch are abroad.

LONDON :

Printed for W. KENNERSLY, near *St. Paul's.* 1755.

(Price Six-pence.)

Pastoral Pimlico. Society nymphs and gallants at the Waterworks. The building on the left is probably Jenny's Whim.

16

The Ranelagh Rotunda.

Ranelagh

The 'Pimlico playground', already thriving, received a massive boost when Ranelagh Gardens opened on its western fringe. It all began with the building of the Royal Hospital, between 1682 and 1692. Tradition ascribed the choice of location to Nell Gwyn, a local lass with some influence over Charles II; and though the point has been disputed a large sign outside the Nell Gwyn public house, just over the Stone Bridge (which carried what is now Pimlico Road across the river Westbourne) boldly proclaimed the connection with the royal favourite until well into the nineteenth century. Her mother Helena lived at the Neat Houses, and died there in 1679: 'sitting near the waterside at her house by the Neat Houses at Chelsea, [she] fell into the water accidentally and was drowned'. Malicious tongues suggested that Mistress Gwyn's demise owed as much to alcohol as to water.

Just east of the Royal Hospital, a sumptuous mansion was built by the Hospital Treasurer, Lord Ranelagh. Intended originally as the Treasurer's residence, a considerable amount of Hospital money was diverted to build a house so splendid that Daniel Defoe likened it to Paradise. 'The very Greenhouses and Stables (adorned with Festoons, Urns etc) have an Air of Grandeur not to be seen in many Princes Pallaces', wrote an admiring visitor in 1698. With such praise, it is not surprising that Ranelagh House soon became popular with the nobility, and in 1733 a group of entrepreneurs bought and converted the house and grounds into one of the most fashionable pleasure gardens in Europe. 'The floor is all of beaten princes', wrote Horace Walpole: 'you can't set your foot without treading on a Prince or Duke of Cumberland.' Dominated by a huge round concert-hall known as the Rotunda, Ranelagh was for decades the place to be. High society flocked to its elaborate masquerades and firework displays, to ride in its gondolas, and even to listen to the concerts. The eight-year old Master Mozart gave an organ recital at Ranelagh in 1764; he was billed as 'the most extraordinary Prodigy, the most amazing Genius that has ever appeared in any Age'.

The success of Ranelagh had a spectacular effect on the neighbourhood, which was

fast becoming a sort of permanent funfair. Most famous of the 'sideshows' was the Chelsea Bun House, which had already acquired a considerable reputation before Ranelagh was opened. The buns were, rather alarmingly, described as being 'as flaky and white ... as the flesh of an infant, soft, doughy and slight'. The jovial Mrs Hands presided over the Bun House for sixty years, a mine of local information and a tourist attraction in her own right. Her customers included both George II and George III, but the Bun House's big day was Good Friday, when thousands of city folk began their day out in the country with one of Mrs Hand's hot cross buns. A visit there was seen as 'quite a treat to the Cockneys, and is recommended to all strangers as one of the sights of London'. People rose early in those days. Baking began at 4 am, and the Bun House regularly had 50,000 customers before 8 am on Good Friday. On one day nearly a quarter of a million buns were consumed. Its fifty-foot colonnade was filled with curios, and an array of bizarre models kept the customers queueing qui-

etly: 'the model of the Bun House with painted masquerade figures on two circles turned round by a bird whilst on its perch in a cage', was a favourite.

Nearby Strombolo Gardens, built or rebuilt in 1765 in a field called Little Rumbelo, boasted a 'fine fountain', and was popular as a place to drink tea, which then was still something of a novelty. Strombolo House still stands, on the south side of Pimlico Road, as a plaque in the wall attests. Two pubs near modern Ebury Square catered for a slightly more down-market clientele. One, the Dwarf, was run by a 'jovial pygmy' and one-time comic actor, whose patrons included a visiting party of Cherokee Indians. A dramatic firework display was held there in 1762 to celebrate the birth of the Prince of Wales, and the guests imbibed 'plenty of sound old bright wine and punch like nectar'. The Star and Garter was the venue of an optimistic entrepreneur called Mr Lowe, who in 1763 lured customers with promises of 'an enchanted clock, which absolutely tells

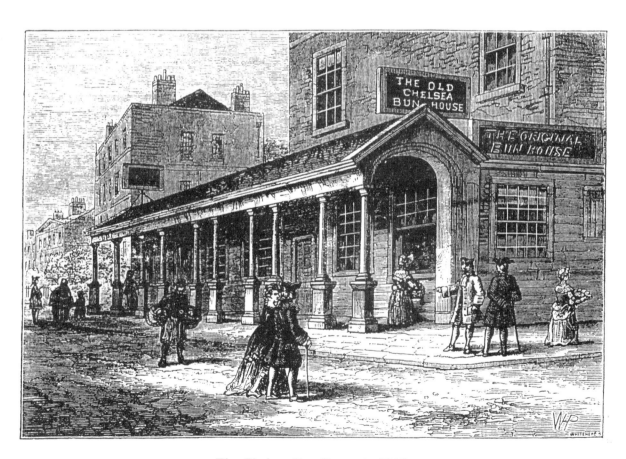

The Chelsea Bun House in 1810.

The Royal Orange Theatre in 1832.

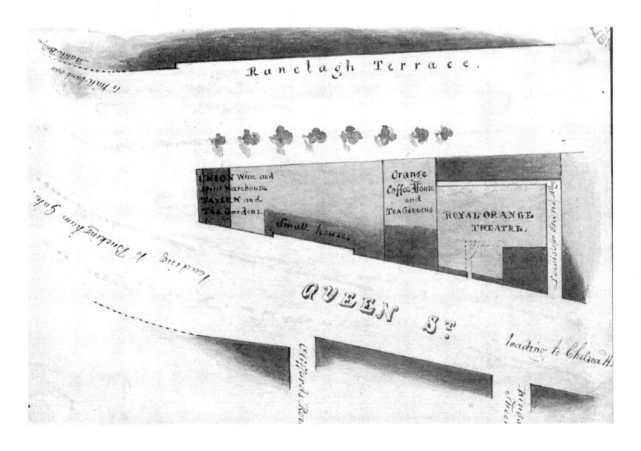

the thoughts of any person in the Company'. Other attractions included 'the astonishing Little Man, only four inches high, pays his respects to the Company and vanishes in a flash of fire'.

Traffic jams on the road to Ranelagh were commonplace - 'we had a stop of six-and-thirty minutes', complained Walpole. Visitors would often travel to Ranelagh in convoy, for the road from town was wild and desolate, and the district's glittering clientele offered rich pickings to footpads and robbers. Lord Onslow's coach was stopped somewhere along the modern Grosvenor Place in 1763 by a solitary footpad, who got away with six guineas. An advert for a 1770 event at Ranelagh assured visitors that 'there will be a Horse Patrole, well armed, continually passing between [Ranelagh] and Hyde Park Corner, and a good Guard at the Back of Chelsea College'. At one point there were 52 privates and six NCOs patrolling the length of Five Fields Row (modern Ebury Street).

But fashion is a fickle thing, and Ranelagh's reputation could not last forever. 'The most insipid place of amusement imaginable', wrote one visitor shortly before it closed its doors in 1803.

With the passing of Ranelagh, the other resorts swiftly declined. The city was getting closer, and the well-to-do were travelling further for their recreation. The Bun House closed in 1839, and was promptly demolished for redevelopment; in the 1820s the Star & Garter made way for Ackermann's Waterproof Cloth Manufactory. Those taverns that survived soon lost their social cachet. The lights of the canal had given way 'to smoke, of which it emits large volumes', and the mechanical curios at Jenny's Whim gave way to 'more violent pleasures such as bull-baiting and dog-fighting, attracting valiant butchers and porters from Clare Market and Westminster, and the gardens lost their fashionable odour'.

Thames Bank on the eve of development.

Attempts were made to revive the fortunes of Pimlico as a resort. The Orange, for example, built on the site of Strombolo's gardens in the Pimlico Road, was described in 1790 as 'eligibly situated in the Road leading from the Waterworks Bridge to the Royal Bunn house at Chelsea'. By the 1830s the pub had extended to include a small auditorium, grandly described as the Royal Orange Theatre. But even such attractions as 'The Assassin' and 'Murder in the Black Forest' failed to attract the wealthy patrons of yore; 'young men of the neighbourhood play about with their dogs between the acts', complained a visitor.

The attractions of the riverbank proved slightly more enduring. At the foot of modern Claverton Street stood the King's Arms Tavern and Tea Gardens, in a house built by the inventor Matthias Koops. It was an attractive building, fitted out with all mod cons: 'an elegant small bow-fronted dwelling-house three stories high, with an observatory, a patent water-closet, strong room, statuary, marble chimney-pieces and a wine cellar'. In 1809, the King's Arms was taken over by an entrepreneur, who tried to evoke the lustre of Ranelagh with a venture which he called the New Ranelagh Tea Gardens. The establishment boasted a resident 'fireworker', Signora Hengier; an event held there in 1810 was said to have been 'a brilliant display of beauty and fashion, and though the gardens were literally crowded to an extreme, everything passed off with the greatest harmony and regularity'. The same reviewer somehow managed not to notice the existence of the London Steel Works next door, and advised the public to book early for the New Ranelagh's next event, 'such being the attractions of this charming spot', but public enthusiasm for the riverbank was waning. An observer of 1827 lamented that Londoners 'who had been for years accustomed to recreate within the chequered shade of Millbank's willows, have been by degrees deprived of that pleasure, as there are now very few trees remaining, and those so scanty of foliage, by being nearly stript of their bark, that the public are no longer induced to tread their sweetly variegated banks'.

^A PROPOSAL

FOR

Raiſing WATER from the River THAMES to ſerve the City and Suburbs of WESTMINSTER, &c.

T is propoſed to raiſe Water from the *Thames* (with Engines working by the Flux and Reflux of the Tide) without prejudicing the Navigation, or any other Part, or Particular belonging to the River, into a Reſervatory rais'd on the higheſt Ground near *Oliver*'s Mount, thence to ſerve the new Buildings, and all other Parts in the City and Suburbs of *Weſtminſter*, and Parts adjacent : The Deſign whereof may be comprehended from the Plan hereunto annex d.

II. THAT, as well for the Eaſe and Advantage of the Work, as for the quick Supplying (in Caſe of any Emergency) the lower Parts of the Town, another Reſervatory ſhall be erected in ſome other Place, the moſt Convenient, to anſwer all Demands from His Majeſty's Palace at St. *James*'s, (if required) and all other Places from thence to *Charing-Croſs* and *Weſtminſter*.

III. THAT in theſe Two or more Reſervatories, (if neceſſary) ſuch a Quantity of Water ſhall be always reſerv'd as will be ſufficient not only to ſupply the ordinary Occaſions of the Inhabitants; but will alſo anſwer all other Calls in Caſe of Fire, the Peſtilence, or any Exigency whatſoever.

IV. THAT, for the Relief of the Labouring Poor, whoſe Livelihood mainly depends on the common Uſes of Water, either in Waſhing, Scowering, &c. ſuch Proviſion ſhall be made as will ſupply their neceſſary Occaſions, and eaſe them of a Burthen which they cannot bear without the greateſt Difficulties.

Laſtly, THAT, for the Advantage and Security of the Proprietors and Adventurers in this Undertaking, no Perſon ſhall be admitted to Sell, or Transfer, any Share, or Shares, until the whole Undertaking is compleated, as is ſet forth in the Petition for an Act of Parliament to carry on a Work ſo uſeful and neceſſary for the Publick Good.

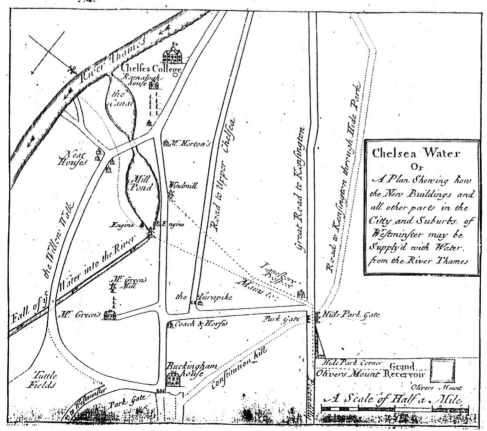

3 The City Approaches

A view of the fire engine of Chelsea Waterworks in 1783.

Fiery Works upon the Riverside

'Coarse grass and rank weeds straggled over all the marshy land in the vicinity', wrote Charles Dickens of Millbank in *David Copperfield*. 'The clash and glare of sundry fiery works upon the riverside arose by night to disturb everything except the heavy and unbroken smoke that poured out of their chimneys. Slimy gaps and causeways winding among old wooden piles, with a sickly substance clinging to the latter like green hair'. Long before Dickens' time, the Thames had become the backbone of an industrial zone that stretched from Westminster to Chelsea, Battersea and beyond. Breweries, boatyards, timberyards, distilleries, vinegar works and a host of other factories were strung out along its banks. The river was highway and rubbish-dump, its waters used for cooling, boiling, washing, processing and drinking.

First to come to Thames Bank, as the Pimlico waterfront was known, was the Chelsea Waterworks, an enterprise that once spread from Chelsea Bridge Road to Warwick Way, from Victoria Station to the river. In 1723, a group of businessmen, anxious to profit from 'the great increase of buildings and inhabitants in and about the City of Westminster', won a grant to supply the huge area from Pall Mall to Kensington with water from the Thames. They persuaded Lord Grosvenor to grant them a 99-year lease of the site on Thames Meadow, and were soon piping water to reservoirs in Hyde and St James' Parks. Business prospered, as well it might, with London expanding on their doorstep and contracts to supply all the royal palaces. The Company had a very good reputation, and were at the forefront of water technology: they introduced the first successful steam pump to London in 1742, on the site of the Grosvenor Hotel at Victoria.

Other industrial development came to Thames Bank during the eighteenth century. A map of 1725 shows that the straight track still known as Turpentine Lane had already been laid out across the land which the Stanley family owned, clearly with a view to some riverside development; but it was many years before Rennie's White Lead works moved onto the site and gave Turpentine Lane its name. Octavius Smith's impressive Thames Bank Distillery was built shortly before 1790: Lutyens and Chippendale Houses, on the Churchill Gardens estate, now occupy the site. The distillery survived a major fire in 1806, and a concerted attempt by both landlord and developer to squeeze it out of the genteel suburb that grew up around it. The enterprise had its own dock, and a sizeable complex of mills, brew-houses and grain stores: it finally closed in 1907.

There were other, smaller, enterprises on the riverbank as well: timber yards and malt-houses, another white lead works. But all of them were dwarfed by Matthias Koops' giant paper mill, built on sixteen acres of garden ground to the west of modern Claverton Street in 1801. Koops had been granted a patent to produce paper from 'straw, hay, thistles, waste and refuse of hemp and flax, and different kinds of wood and bark', and his Patent Straw Paper Company's mill on Thames Bank was probably the largest in the country at that time. It was a wildly ambitious project, which involved, amongst much else, the cutting of a sizeable dock, and Koops' expenditure was lavish: within three years his business had folded.

Koops' business partners included one John Hunter, who persuaded the Grosvenor Estate to be 'lenient' with their ambitious tenant - and his backers too, of course. The Estate obliged, and Hunter found a new partner: Joseph Bramah, ironmaster, inventor and locksmith - 'the ingenious Mr Bramah, whose locks baffle knavery'. Bramah's London Steel Works at Thames Bank were de-

The Thames Bank distillery in 1797.

scribed as 'the chief ornament of this neighbourhood ... [an] amazingly extensive and interesting manufactory'. His visitors at Thames Bank included 'the most powerful emperor in Christendom, Alexander of Russia', but, the Czar's interest notwithstanding, Bramah's sons transferred their enterprise to a more accessible location after their father's death in 1814, and three years later the lease was assigned to John Johnson for development.

On the Urban Fringe

The Neat House Gardens by 1820 had become the classic urban fringe: a mixture of unpleasant industry on the waterfront, some haphazard and half-built cottages, and a range of increasingly seedy taverns and resorts. The gardeners were still there, of course, but London society no longer came to sample the produce, or to wander along the Willow Walk to the Monster or Jenny's Whim. 'Nothing better than a waterlogged marsh', one veteran recalled with distaste, 'redolent of the decaying cabbage and other leaves festering in their own rottenness'.

The Willow Walk, once a pleasant stroll from town, was now described as 'flanked on each side by a filthy ditch, the filth hidden by the duck weed'. Improbably enough, the Walk formed part of the coronation route of George IV in 1821. The former Prince Regent had become so unpopular that his advisers decided to smuggle him out of Westminster Abbey by the back way to avoid the hostile crowds. All went well until the royal party reached 'a broad deep canal, full of water and mud, over which lay an old wooden bridge, stopped up at its entrance with strong barricadoes'. The barricadoes were duly removed, and the procession crossed in safety, although 'the planks creaked, shook, bent and were all in great holes'. The King was described as 'horribly nervous' throughout the journey, 'and kept continually calling to the officers of the escort to keep well up to the carriage windows'.

It seems that the King did not call in at the bear-garden, situated about half-way along the Walk (roughly on the site of today's Hamilton House Hotel in Warwick Way). Known as 'Billy's Cabin', it had been the abode of 'Slender Billy', alias William Heberfield. 'His dwelling was suitable to concealment, and garrisoned by buffers, so as to render it impregnable to sudden attack'. Those who scaled the fences found themselves within 'a menagerie for beasts of almost every description', including bears. Slender Billy was hanged in 1812, framed on a forgery charge, but not before he had become a popular figure with the pupils of Westminster School, who looked upon Tothill Fields and the Neat House Gardens as one huge playground. Lord Albemarle, a Westminster pupil, remembered Billy as 'a good humoured, amusing fellow': a man who could be relied upon to supply schoolboys with the right dog 'to hunt a duck, draw a badger or pin a bull'.

Westminster pupils mingled freely with the area's wilder inhabitants - even though, as Albemarle said, they were 'not of that class with which ladies would wish their darling boys to associate'. Caleb Baldwin was another popular figure - a bull-baiter who could catch a dog tossed by a bull's horns before it touched the ground. And if a boy fancied a spot of shooting, he could always pop over to Mother Hubbard's and select a piece from that lady's arsenal of dodgy weapons. Her collection included a remarkable firearm which fired around corners.

Invitation to the coronation, 1821.

The coronation of George IV. The King's arrival at Westminster Abbey was considerably more dignified than his departure.

A Fortunate Marriage

The manor of Ebury changed hands many times after it was taken from the Abbey, eventually passing to a London scrivener called Alexander Davies. In 1676 Davies married off his twelve-year-old daughter Mary to a Cheshire baronet called Sir Thomas Grosvenor. It was a match that sealed the fortunes of this lucky family, for it gave them freehold ownership of a huge area to the west of London just as the city was expanding that way. By 1770, a large slice of the Ebury Manor had been developed as Mayfair, and with their wealth came steadily

Mary Davies.

increasing status: Baron Grosvenor in 1761, Earl Grosvenor in 1784, and later Marquess (1831) and Duke (1874) of Westminster.

Once Mayfair had been built, the Grosvenors began to consider developing other parts of Mary Davies' dowry. The building of Vauxhall Bridge and Vauxhall Bridge Road in 1816 opened up the southern area of their estate, and within a few years the adjacent Tothill Fields had been laid out in streets. Residential development on Millbank and the riverside was somewhat retarded by the building of the Millbank Penitentiary, begun in 1812. Although intended to be a model of its kind, the prison was not a success, for it was 'happily situated in a swamp, below the tide level of the river', as one critic sarcastically observed. Inmates likened it to Devil's Island. The prison survived until 1890: the Tate Gallery now occupies the site. The Grosvenors' own house on Millbank was demolished for redevelopment, but with such a neighbour their plans were not ambitious. Much of the work was given to one John Johnson, a speculative builder then busy all over London. Contemporaries were at first impressed by his endeavours: in 1822 he was said to be 'considerably improving' the area around Smith Square. His houses were small, however, and poorly drained, and the development was not completed; they were probably the 'carcasses of houses, inauspiciously begun and never finished', that Dickens discovered rotting away on Millbank.

Various schemes were put forward for developing the Neat House Gardens. The draughtsman John Gwyn had dreams of incorporating the district in a new city of broad, straight roads. A highway was to be built from Islington to the Thames at Ranelagh, and the hinterland was to be laid out in a grid of grand streets. The Prince Regent himself, town planner extraordinary and John Nash's patron, was also said to have had 'plans' for transforming the area, but until the 1820s the Grosvenor Estate had little incentive to do so. The fertility of the land ensured that they received a healthy rental from the gardeners for very little outlay, while the cost of preparing the floodplain for development was huge; and anyway the Estate was preoccupied with developments elsewhere.

The only building on the Neat House Gardens occurred on land that did not belong to the Grosvenors. St George's Row, a terrace of small cottages just south of Ebury Bridge, was built soon after the Waterworks on land belonging to the Stanley family. (The district

Police patrol at Millbank Prison.

became part of the new parish of St George Hanover Square in 1725, which may explain the name). At the end of the century, a cluster of little houses were built around modern Garden Row and Moreton Street, on land that still belonged to Westminster Abbey. Joseph Bramah was another developer to spot the potential for building on the Neat House Gardens. He proposed various schemes for draining the land, and as early as 1805 he was suggesting to his landlords that a 'good road ... would tend greatly to the advantage of Lord Grosvenor's estate in that Neighbourhood'. He urged that the existing lanes be widened, and proposed to build some workers' cottages ('fourth-rate houses') along Baker's Lane, but he failed to enthuse his landlord.

Bramah's successor at Thames Bank was John Johnson, the Millbank builder. At first, like Bramah, Johnson had big plans for the whole district. In 1819 he proposed extending his streets across the Neat House Gardens to Vauxhall Bridge Road and to the

Monster, but the Estate, which by now was finalising plans to build the Grosvenor Canal when the Waterworks company lease was up, refused to grant Johnson any land that might allow him to extend the dock which he had inherited from Koops and Bramah. Johnson pressed ahead with a much more modest development, but even this was only partly completed. For, right from the start, Johnson found himself faced with the implacable opposition of the gardeners.

The Gardeners' Last Stand

Some of the Neat House gardeners did very well from their trade, particularly nurserymen such as the Terwin family, who left a charitable bequest to 'the Neat House poor', but most of them were far from wealthy. Lord Albemarle described the gardeners' homes as 'wretched hovels, to which were attached small plots of swampy ground which served the poor inhabitants for gardens, and were separated from each other by ditches'. Many of them were tenants-at-will, with very

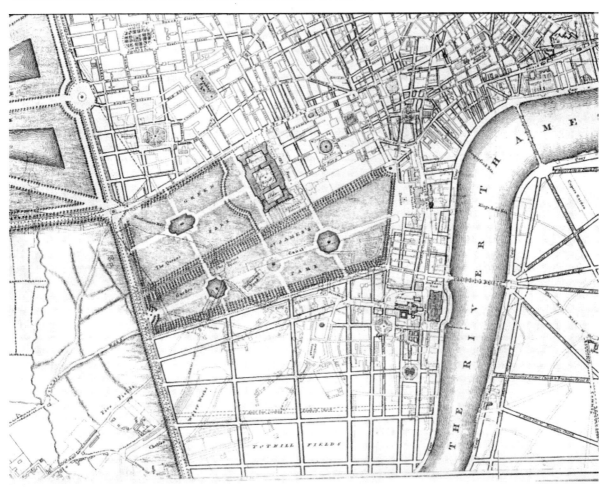

Detail from John Gwyn's 'London and Westminster Improved', 1766.

little security, and they had everything to lose from Johnson's development. The roads were staked out in their presence on 1 April 1820, but the gardeners, as an Estate official diplomatically put it, were 'not quite Cordial to the Business'.

Led, it seems, by a tenant-at-will named Cook, they managed to delay completion of the roads for well over a year. Cook proved to be quite an ingenious adversary. Ever since Koops' venture, the gardeners had been told by the Estate that they 'were not to put any Crops on the Ground which would last beyond the year', but Cook had planted licquorice - a three-year crop - and despite having been given notice to quit by Christmas, he claimed that the Estate 'could not dispossess him in less than three years'. In July, Johnson complained to the Estate 'of the inconvenience and the injury' he was sustaining due to the gardeners' opposition and demands for adequate recompense. Only one gardener, who had been given land elsewhere, did not oppose the road. The

gardeners found other allies: in November John White, owner of the timber-yard at the mouth of the Tyburn, withdrew his consent to a new bridge across the little river 'as he would not embroil himself in a dispute with the gardeners'. Work by Johnson's men on a new ditch parallel to the Tyburn was stopped in December 'on account of some Cabbage plants ... for which Cook would require compensation'.

Johnson did succeed in building Thames Parade, a row of pleasant stucco houses on Grosvenor Road that still stand today. Elsewhere, however, Johnson's plans never recovered from the antagonism of the gardeners. By 1825, there was just one terrace of workers' houses along the line of Johnson's Place, and a few cottages along Ranelagh Road. In October that year, Johnson sold his lease to Thomas Cubitt. Cubitt, no doubt aware of Johnson's problems with the gardeners, compensated them generously, and allowed them to remove their sheds and outbuildings. He re-let the gardens to one Mr

Johnson's development on Thames Bank. The bow-fronted house in the background was the New Ranelagh Tea Gardens.

Besmocked gardeners at work on the banks of the Tyburn, 1808.
John White's timber yard is in the foreground.

Martin, who continued to use the land until it was needed for building purposes: he finally left soon after 1840. A small pocket of market garden ground survived for a few years longer, on land belonging to the Waterworks at the northern end of modern Peabody Avenue. A curious twist, for this same plot, centuries earlier, had been the garden of the Neyte itself; the very first, and the very last, of the famous Neat House Gardens.

4 The Building of Pimlico

Thames Parade

The Southern Estate

For some time past, the Grosvenor Estate had been seriously considering developing the land that became 'Belgravia'. The canal of the Chelsea Waterworks, they realised, had a great deal of potential as a route for transporting heavy, bulky building materials, and well before the lease was up in 1823, the Estate had laid detailed plans to convert their filter-beds and reservoirs into a proper canal. By 1825, lock-gates had been fitted, and a large 'basin' constructed on the site of Victoria Station (the Grosvenor Basin public house, opposite the station on Wilton Road, survived until 1926: a name to mystify travellers and locals alike). The Estate had no shortage of takers for builders' wharves, warehouses and factories along the new Grosvenor Canal. Most of the wharves around the Basin were quickly let to builders on the Estate; but although Commercial Road, now Ebury Bridge Road, was opened in 1827 to service them, many wharves at the Chelsea end were not let until the 1840s.

John Johnson's mediocre achievements may have convinced the Estate of the need to find a developer of ambition and proven ability to develop their 'southern estate'. They turned to Thomas Cubitt, an ambitious young speculative builder who had already made a name for himself with developments in the Grays Inn Road and further north in the 'stockbroker villages' of Highbury and Stoke Newington, and was in the throes of negotiating some major projects with the Bedford Estate in Bloomsbury. In August 1824, Cubitt

The new Grosvenor Canal.
Belgrave Bridge (now Eccleston Bridge) was
built by Thomas Cubitt.

This was the beginning of Belgravia, the development that made both Cubitt's fortune and his name. Cubitt was by no means the only developer at work in Belgravia, but he was the biggest and the most influential, and contemporaries were in no doubt about his achievement. 'A fairer wreath than Wren's should crown thy brow - He raised a dome - a town unrivalled thou!', enthused an awe-struck resident. Cubitt's interest in Pimlico began early in 1825, when he was given the lease on land for some small sites in Vauxhall Bridge Road and north of the canal basin, where he took a lot of wharfside property. In July, he signed the agreement to develop the Neat House Gardens (now known simply as 'the Neathouses'). His 'take' was divided into three plots, of which 'A', (31 acres south and east of modern Lupus and Claverton Streets) was deemed to be the most valuable, as its river-frontage meant that industrial development was always a possibility should his plans fail. The twenty acres of 'B' were on the Vauxhall Bridge Road part of the site; 'C', twenty-nine acres, accounted for the rest.

entered into an agreement with the Estate to build new houses to the value of £50,000 on nineteen acres between Belgrave Square and the King's Road.

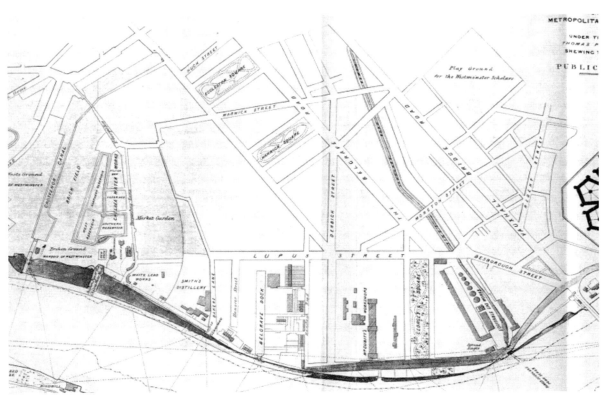

The building of Pimlico: Lupus Street, St George's Drive and the Squares had been laid out by
1843, but the western part of Pimlico had yet to be developed.

Thomas Cubitt.

In October, Cubitt bought out the remaining years of John Johnson's fifteen-and-a-half acre lease, and at the same time was negotiating with the Stanley family and the heirs of Henry Wise, the two other substantial landowners in the Neathouses. Cubitt made a deliberate policy of cornering land in the Neathouses, for, as he said, this allowed him to ensure 'that a uniform style may be kept in the Buildings and Roads'. It also put him in an unusually powerful position relative to all three landowners, even the Grosvenor Estate; he was able to persuade them to make many complex land exchanges so that their holdings were reorganised to fit his street system - and, when the building industry went into its periodic troughs, to renegotiate the terms of his agreements.

Raising the Lowlands

Cubitt's first task was to raise the ground level. It was a formidable job: in some places at least four feet of 'made ground' was needed just to bring the land up to basement level. Cubitt himself estimated that it took over 180,000 cubic yards to raise the level of Eccleston Square alone. Huge quantities of infill - spoil from the docks, but also road scrapings, demolition waste and general refuse - were brought from all over London, mostly by river, to the canal, to Johnson's dock, and to other spots along the riverbank where, as a local official lugubriously observed, 'preparations have been made for

Eccleston Square: the beginnings of Cubitt's Pimlico.

Looking east from Cubitt's works. The 'viaducts' of pavement vaults mark out the roadlines. Miss Dangerfield's public house, the Perseverance, stands in splendid isolation behind the shrubbery of St George's, as yet unbuilt.

facilitating the unloading of Barges bringing earth to raise the contiguous low Lands'. By 1834, enough work had been done to convince the Commission of Sewers that this flood-prone stretch of river-front was so much raised 'that not any Danger is to be apprehended'. Closely connected with the infilling was the laying of 'numerous new and long lines of sewers', for which Cubitt was praised in 1843. They served both to drain the land, and the houses that were to be built on it - an idea that seems obvious now but which was very unusual at the time. The Tyburn (now the King's Scholars' Pond Sewer), was arched over gradually, mostly at Cubitt's expense, and was largely finished by November 1844.

'It is in the first stages of forming a new district that attention is required to provide good Public ways', wrote Cubitt in 1836. In 1828 he began work on Eccleston Square and Belgrave Road 'to form a good communication from London to Vauxhall Bridge and the Thames Bank', and contracted to

Pimlico porticoes: the southern end of St George's Drive (c1900).

build 'two substantial Brick Bridges over the Canal'. Eccleston Bridge was finally finished in 1832, St George's Bridge in 1837; both were widened in the 1840s. Ebury Bridge, the 'Wooden Bridge', lay too far to the west of Cubitt's main estates to be of much interest to him; although described as 'dangerously decayed' in 1828, the bridge was not replaced until 1847-50. Although the Grosvenors saw the district south of the canal as a 'secondary, largely independent development for the area rather than a continuation of prime residential development from the north', Cubitt himself was understandably keen to link his Neathouses development with Belgravia, which was already becoming a highly desirable neighbourhood. Pimlico's diagonal grid plan is largely dictated by a desire to show that 'South Belgravia' was indeed an extension of Belgravia proper: thus Eccleston Street continues southwards as Belgrave Road, and Elizabeth Street in Pimlico becomes St George's Drive.

Existing routes were retained to a surprising extent, perhaps because of the piecemeal way in which Pimlico was developed. Thus Willow Walk remains, as Warwick Way, Cross Street as Lupus Street, the track to Johnson's

estate as Denbigh Street and Claverton Street. Baker's Lane (or Distillery Lane) was later straightened out to form Sutherland Street; tiny Turpentine Lane, on the edge of Cubitt's Pimlico, has survived with its name unchanged. Many streets were named after the Grosvenor family's various estates and titles. The crop of West Country names around Wilton Road was intended as a compliment to the wife of the first Marquess, daughter of Earl Wilton who had huge estates in Wiltshire and Dorset. Other streets were named after places in Warwickshire, where the Wise family had property. Although Alderney Street was originally named Stanley Street, in recognition of the Stanley family, the only name to have survived is the Stanley Arms pub in Lupus Street.

Portico-Westminster-Italianate

On the site of Dolphin Square and Pimlico School, Cubitt established a building works of impressive proportions, praised by the *Builder* in 1845 for 'extent, comprehensiveness and completeness'. A sizeable brickworks converted clay quarried near the Grosvenor Canal, and the establishment also included a sawmill and a joinery, a marble

The bigger houses were slow to sell. St George's Drive and Belgrave Road in the late 19th century.

Number One Pimlico Road (demolished in 1928).

works, a smithy for wrought-iron work, and an engineering works that boasted a ten-ton crane.

Cubitt seems to have been popular with his large workforce. Facilities at Thames Bank included a reading-room and lending library - 'Mr Cubitt's Workmen's Library'. He reduced the working week to a mere 58 hours, and plied his employees with subsidised coffee, to the consternation of the local publicans ('the beer men were not allowed to go round in the mornings'). He did not succeed in stopping the determined drinker, however. 'We advise Smith, of the bricklayers, not to drop in so often at the Marquis of Westminster and there to take his drains on the sly; and May, of the smith's not to pay so much attention to Miss Dangerfield at the Perseverance', counselled a nosey colleague in 1839.

Cubitt's men laid out the streets and the sewers, and made up some of the vaults. He decided on the size and number of houses in each street, and carefully restricted their use. He sometimes provided elevations, and certainly insisted on a good deal of design uniformity. Although many distinguished architects began their careers in Cubitt's drawing office, the house style was set by Cubitt himself - with more than a little influence from the ground landlords. If one man can be said to have had more influence than any other over house design in Pimlico, it was probably the second Marquess of Westminster, who inherited the estate in 1845. He was very keen on stucco, and the balcony-over-doric-portico so characteristic of Pimlico house design has been dubbed 'Portico Westminster Italianate' by Hermione Hobhouse.

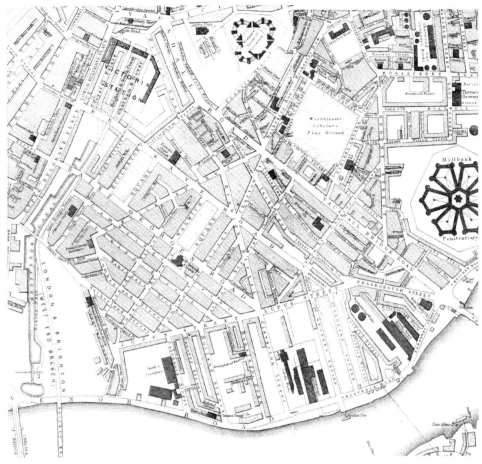

Mr Cubitt's district in 1862.

The Stucco Spreads

Actual building work was undertaken by many different contractors, who took plots varying in size from a single house to an entire block, which they developed as and when they were able to. Building was therefore sporadic, and groups of finished houses would stand in odd, up-market hamlets for years before the gaps were filled. It was a shrewd move: for although Cubitt supplied his contractors with credit and materials - in fact seems to have insisted on it ('it should be observed that my houses are not subject to the risk of the usual mode of Building as the work is all prepared at Thames Bank in the Shops', he told his insurers in 1841), he himself was insulated against a great deal of the risk. Many small builders went out of business during the building slump of the 1850s. Cubitt was sympathetic - 'you may now pass from [Belgravia] to Thames Bank without the sound of the hammer - the money market has made very sad work among the builders - many of them are quite stopped

and in difficulties, and all of them are greatly depressed' - but the risk was not his own.

Building began in the 1830s, with a few houses along Belgrave Road and in Eccleston Square. Cubitt took trouble to find and accommodate the right tenants, but development of the larger houses in the squares and along the two main streets was very slow. At the time of Cubitt's death in 1855, 48% of the houses in Belgrave Road, and 42% of those in St George's Road, were still unoccupied. The north side of Eccleston Square was still unfinished, and Warwick Square was less than half built. Few houses in St George's Square were built until the 1850s, and building work continued until well into the 1870s.

Development of the smaller streets went far more smoothly. The Marquis of Westminster was let in 1838, and from this point the sea of houses spread along Warwick Way and Lillington Street during the 1840s. In 1847, building work began south of War-

wick Square and west of St George's Drive. The northern end of Alderney and Cambridge Streets was taken by 1852, and by 1856 both streets were complete, but the area west, to Sutherland Street and beyond, was not finished until the mid-1860s. The north side of Lupus Street was built during the 1850s, but south of this point very little building work was done until the rest of the area was completed. Johnson's estate was not rebuilt until after 1851 - in that year Ranelagh Road was described as 'a very unapproachable district'. The building of the Embankment was one of Cubitt's triumphs. After years of official prevarication, he pre-empted the authorities by building up his share of the waterfront himself. Work was completed in 1854, and the rest of the Embankment 'saved' by the decision to build Chelsea Bridge.

Cubitt developed a close working relationship with Prince Albert and Queen Victoria, for whom he built Osborne House on the Isle of Wight. He was involved in many other building projects too, but nowhere did he have so much control as he did in Pimlico. His men not only made but maintained and lit the roads, and took away the refuse, and when in 1856 control of 'Mr Cubitt's District' was handed over to the local authority - the Vestry of St George Hanover Square - the Vestry retained Cubitt's organisation to service it. Soon afterwards, the Vestry built a palatial local town hall at number 1, Pimlico Road to service the new district; opened in 1862, the complex included a Board Room, a wharf, three cottages and a residence for the Surveyor, all behind a grand stucco facade of which Mr Cubitt would certainly have approved.

Cubitt was a shrewd man. His estate was valued at nearly a million pounds, and his 'eye to the main chance', as Charles Knight put it, was proverbial amongst his contemporaries. But his brand of 'enlightened self-interest' was very popular with the Victorians, and he won the affection and respect of his workforce and his clients alike. 'A better, kinder-hearted or more simple, unassuming man never breathed', lamented Queen Victoria on his death in 1855.

The Cubitt family's connections with Pimlico did not stop with the death of the developer. The family owned a lot of freehold property in Pimlico, and Thomas' eldest son George built the 'iron church' of All Saints on Grosvenor Road in 1860. In 1865, his sister Lucy built herself a substantial house at the southern end of Warwick Square. Miss Lucy Cubitt accepted her father's mantle as 'lady of the manor' with good grace. Until her death in 1897, her house was 'a centre of hospitality and good cheer'. Annual flower shows were held on her lawn, and 'Miss Cubitt's Days' - outings in the country for the beleaguered parish workers of St Gabriel's - 'became a byword for summer gaiety and escape from a crowded parish'. In 1995, William Franke's statue of Thomas Cubitt was erected at the southern end of St George's Drive. It was unveiled by the Duke of Westminster, a fitting tribute to the man who did so much to make the Duke's family amongst the wealthiest in the country.

5 South Belgravia?

The Grand Junction Waterworks in 1828. Water was drawn from beneath the floating hut, marked (1). (2) marks the mouth of the Ranelagh Sewer (the sweet river Westbourne no more).

The Great Stink

Pimlico in 1887 was described as 'one of the most healthy districts of London'. This was, in large measure, due to Cubitt's purpose-built drainage system, which was well ahead of its time. The district's drinking water, however, was drawn at first from the river Thames just off Grosvenor Road, and dubious stuff it was too. Cubitt was very aware of this, and in 1843 he proposed a system of mains drainage for the whole city, but meanwhile he could do little about the state of the river itself - or the quality of the drinking water that arrived in his new houses.

The Chelsea Waterworks, which drew its water from the middle of the river, had a good reputation for the quality of its water. Not so the Grand Junction Waterworks, which in 1820 positioned itself almost next door. The Grand Junction had promised its 7,000 customers wholesome, fresh water from the distant rural streams of west Middlesex. They were not surprisingly upset to discover that the supply actually came from the Thames, and from the mouth of the Ranelagh Sewer at that. Grand Junction water, it seems, was enough to turn one to drink: 'the very sight of a jug of Grand Junction water serves as an excuse for a

glassful of spirits, to qualify the effects it may have on the stomach,' explained one tippler.

Unfortunately for the Grand Junction Company, the area it served included Harley Street, whose influential medical residents were unimpressed by the liquid that arrived in their homes. 'Scarcely a week passes that I am not presented with a leech, a shrimp-like skipping insect, near an inch in length; a small red delicate worm ... or some other animalculae, and the water is mostly opaline, muddy or otherwise impure', fulminated Dr Hooper, author of the *Medical Directory*. Threatened with Parliamentary action in 1829, the company found a purer supply of water upstream.

Technology saved the Chelsea company from a similar fate, for in the same year James Simpson, the company engineer, introduced the first successful slow sand filter bed. It was a great success, and was copied widely throughout the world. Simpson ran his own engineering works in Eccleston Street and later in Belgrave Road; when the railway was built, the firm transferred to Grosvenor Road, where it survived until well into this cen-

tury. The Chelsea Waterworks had lost the core of its operations in 1825, when the Grosvenor Estate took its original 89-acre lease in hand to build the canal. The company had been acquiring bits of freehold and leasehold land on both sides, however, and as late as 1844 was still landing 5,000 tons of materials a year from the river; but in 1852 an Act of Parliament ended its right to draw water from the urban waters of the Thames, and the company moved its works to Surbiton. It says something for the quality of engineer Simpson's new filter-beds that the Chelsea Waterworks was able to draw Thames water for as long as it did, for the riverbank at Pimlico was in 1845 described as 'covered in red worms, called 'bloodworm', which give the red appearance to the shores of the River. They are attributed to the sewage'.

In a lecture given to Pimlico residents in 1857, the local Medical Officer of Health held the bloodworm responsible for the 'offensive smell with gaseous bubbles' that emanated from the Grosvenor Canal, and no doubt for the 'intolerable stench' that the King's Scholars' Pond Sewer inflicted on the inhabitants of Lupus Street. As *Punch* drily remarked, 'the Banks of the Thames are rich in Deposits'. A 'gaseous discharge' in 1852 from the sewer in Warwick Way killed five people, and the great cholera outbreak two years later saw deaths in practically every street in Pimlico.

Matters came to a head in 1858, the year of the 'Great Stink'. In July, a *Punch* correspondent noticed a man 'at the foot of Chelsea Bridge taking fish out of the Thames with his hands, and putting them into a bucket of fresh water. They were only just saved in time, as they were all but poisoned with the filth'. A short way downstream, the stench in the House of Commons was getting up the Honourable Members' noses. MPs ran gasp-

The Western Pumping Station in 1904.

Old Chelsea Bridge.

ing from committee rooms clutching hand-kerchiefs - 'the Noes will have it', quipped *Punch* - and raced their way through the legislative timetable. The engineer in charge of ventilation for the Houses of Parliament declared that 'he could no longer be held responsible for the health of the House', and came up with an intriguing proposal to run a chimney up the side of Big Ben to burn off the noxious gases. Fears of plague were rife. One frightened MP warned that 'families were already flying from the Metropolis to avoid the coming pestilence, and a complete panic was commencing'. Bad smells concentrated the legislative mind wonderfully, and within a few days Prime Minister Disraeli rushed through a Bill empowering the newly-formed Metropolitan Board of Works to sort the situation out.

The Board's engineer, Sir Joseph Bazalgette, solved the problem by building two huge sewers on either side of the river to intercept the city's waste; these remain the arteries of London's sewage system to this day. Bazalgette's solution not merely removed the fear of pestilence from Pimlico, but endowed the district with its most prominent landmark: the tower of the Western Pumping Station, completed in 1875, standing beside the pump-house like a cathedral campanile, and described by his contemporaries as 'a most conspicuous and beautiful object'. It complemented the 105-foot 'italianated' square chimney of Cubitt's works just upstream, which was only right, since Cubitt had anticipated Bazalgette's scheme by a generation.

Work and Play

Cubitt's Pimlico was what would nowadays be called a 'green field development'. It did not grow up around an existing nucleus, but looked to the areas around it to supply most of the services it required. Churches were provided, a few pubs, and a limited amount of shopping space; but there was no provision at first for schools, or public meeting-places, or public open space. These things came later, as the district matured and the needs of its people became clearer.

The need for open space was soon appreciated. Pimlico's three squares were private places, maintained by subscription - 'they are very safe places for the children,' wrote Cubitt, 'and on that account much preferred to public Walks' - but, apart from the little riverfront garden by St George's Square, the new district had no public open space at all.

Cubitt was, however, very conscious of the demand for it. In 1843 he told the Metropolitan Commissioners that a formal park on Battersea Fields would be very successful: 'the number of people who would take advantage of it would ... be immense'.

Battersea Fields was a wild and boggy tract of common land where London's poor went out to play. A Sunday ferry took passengers from the 'White Ferry House', near the Royal Hospital, on the north bank, to the 'Red House' on the south. The southern pub was famous for its 'flounders breakfasts, sucking-pig dinners, pigeon-shooting and whores', and the middle classes found the freedom of the fields offensive. Here, according to Cubitt, 'the idle and dissolute of both sexes ... while away their time in sports of the lowest and most vulgar kind'. On his suggestion, the Government eventually bought the land, and decided not only to transform the marshy Battersea Fields into a public park, but to build a bridge to serve it.

This was 'enlightened self-interest' at its most overt. Cubitt himself not only owned much of the land at Battersea Fields; he also had another development at Clapham Park. The new bridge thus not only catered for the park-hungry multitudes of Pimlico, but brought Clapham that much closer to the city too. Progress was slow: work did not begin on either Chelsea Bridge or Battersea Park for several years, but both were finally opened in 1858; on March 26, the Queen took a brace of princesses across the bridge to take a turn in the park.

Chelsea Bridge delighted everyone. 'The new bridge appears like a fairy structure', wrote the *Illustrated London News*, 'with its beautiful towers, gilded and painted to resemble light coloured bronze and crowned with large globular lamps, diffusing sunny light all around'. The park, too, proved popular, although the Red House was closed down by the government, and the types of recreation duly regulated by bye-law. The ferry ceased

The Pimlico Literary Institute.

PIMLICO ROOMS,

Warwick St, Pimlico. One Week only

Monday, Sept. 19 to Saturday 24

First Seats 1s Second 6d Third 3d

Commencing 8. Open 7 : 30. Children under Twelve and Schools Half-price to First and Second Seats.

Songs & Duets, Musical Selections by the BAND

M. BENOTTI'S COLOSSAL

DIORAMA

OF

MEDITERRANEAN COAST AND CONTINENTAL SCENERY

In the first instance we shall skirt the shores of ancient Iberia, visit the famous Rock at Gibraltar, steam over the classic waters of the Mediterranean, peep into Malta; look upon Alexandria; steam up the Nile to Boulac and Cairo; run into the Grecian Archipelago, touch the Island of Tenedos, pass into the Dardanelles, reach the Golden Horn, land at Tophana, and wander through the tortuous streets of Stamboul, and in the second portion we shall return through sunny Italy; visiting beautiful Venice; travel along the lovely valleys of Switzerland, over the Alps, and reaching Paris at night.

SYNOPSIS OF SCENERY:

South Western Railway Station. Departure of the Mail Train for Southampton—8 p.m. Preparations for the Voyage—The Peninsular and Oriental Company's Steamer clearing the Docks.

Isle of Wight and Osborne House. Passing the Town of Cowes—Beautiful View of the Needles by moonlight; the most famous landmarks upon our coast.

Crossing the Bay of Biscay. Nearing the Berlingas Rocks—Blowing a Gale—The Rolling Sea—Lightning, Thunder, and Rain; Steam issuing from the funnel of steamer—A Fine Painting.

Portuguese Town of Cintra. Standing on the declivity of Sierra de Cintra and surrounded by ruined buildings of Moorish and Christian architecture—Glorious Sunset.

British Fleet in TRAFALGAR BAY—Corner of Europe and Africa—Battle of Trafalgar—"England expects every man to do his duty!" Death of Nelson. RIVER TAGUS—Early morning—Busy scene.

The Mouldering Ramparts of Tarifa look as if they could be battered down with oranges! The green hills swelling into Lofty Mountains with here and there a white Village or Watch Tower.

The Granite Key to the Land-Locked Mediterranean. We are now opposite to that grim rock of Gibraltar which we took with so much trouble, but which the combined forces of Europe on shore and afloat, have hitherto failed to take from us again—A Story of the Siege of 1782.

New and Old Town of Algiers. Handsome Arcades, Spacious, Elegant, and Regular streets, the Inhabitants Moors, French, Arabs, Jews, Maltese, Germans, and Italians.

Island of Pantelaria. Sunset—Calm—Evening—Distant view of the Town. Pretty Native Craft.

Malta and Valetta. Another of the stepping-stones upon which John Bull rests, with his seven-league boots, in his progress to and from his possessions in India.

Alexandria by Night seen from the deck of the Steamer—This View is pronounced one of the Most Beautiful ever executed—The Donkey boys. An amusing incident.

The Egyptian Canal, or Mahmoudieh—a journey between Alexandria and Cairo—The far off Pyramids in the Valley of the Nile. Frightful Sacrifice of 30,000 Lives.

Night on the Nile. Port of Boulack—One mile from the Egyptian Capital. Fires burning on the Shore.

Grand Cairo and the Citadel. The Last of the Mamelukes—They repaired for the last time in all their splendour to the fortress, and paid their congratulations to the pacha, then turned to take their leave. But the gates had been closed, and a murderous fire of musketry was opened upon them, till man and horse lay heaped in one promiscuous carnage. The City by night—Thousand lights from the various buildings lend a beauty to the scene that can only be felt but not described.

Night Before the Battle. Reminiscences of the Campaign of 1857—"Dreaming of Home!"—The Highlander sleeping—Bivouack Fire—The Vision—Beautiful Effect—The Siege and the Relief—Three Splendid Tableaux.

Entering the Dardanelles and running into the Sea of Marmora, the Gorgeous Panorama of the

City of the Sultan! opens to the view of the traveller in all its unrivalled loveliness. The Enchanted Castle of the glorious Calif, and the all-powerful Sovereign of Islam—Surprise felt by the Oriental Traveller on landing, his brain full of the "Arabian Nights' Entertainments," his eyes dazzled by flashing minarets, glistening walls, and darkly waving trees, when he sets foot in streets filled with offal, filth, and crowds of ravening dogs.

Galata and the Fire Tower. Founded by the Genoese—Residence of European merchants—A wonderful change takes place in this scene—Day, Night, and Illumination.

The Golden Horn. The water glistening in the sunlight and bearing vessels from every country under heaven, and the gilded boats passing to and fro with the fair daughters of Stamboul, the snowy folds of the yackmack concealing all save a pair of dark oriental eyes.

View from Cassim Pasha. Coffee House—Now a Frank may enter a Turkish restaurant, he may smoke his tchibouque with a Turk, attend military parade, lounge about the precincts of the Seraglio or the Mosque, without the slightest molestation.

The Bazaar. The Bazaars of Constantinople are most interesting to the stranger.

Valley of Sweetwaters. Full-robed and bearded Turks, cross-legged on their carpets, sipping coffee and sherbet, and smoking the never-absent tchibouque.

Summer Palace on the Bosphorus. The effects produced in this magnificent painting are truly marvellous.

Mount Vesuvius in Eruption. The nearest possible approach to reality—Much visited by Tourists, owing to the beauty of the surrounding scenery, and because it is in the heart of Italy

Silver Illumination of St. Peter's. The whole of this immense church—its columns, capitals, cornices and pediments—the beautiful swell of the lofty dome, towering into heaven, are all designed in lines of fire.

Grand Effect—Splendid Interior View! Adorned with plates of the richest marbles, copies of the most celebrated paintings and statues—The great bell solemnly tolling, summoning the inhabitants of Rome to the Celebration of the Adoration of the Cross

Magnificent Display of Fireworks from the Tower of St. Angelo. To produce anything approaching this suparb pyrotechnical exhibition has hitherto failed in this country Here will be introduced as near an approximation to the original as it is possible for the Artist and Mechanic, combined, to invent.

Venice, the City of the Sea. One of the noblest, most famous, and singular cities in the world.

Across the Alps by the Mont Cenis Railway. Reaching an elevation of 6,776 feet above the sea—Simplon, named after a famous mountain of Switzerland, and lying at the foot of the Lepontine Alps The AVALANCHE—Startling Effect.

Paris: Hotel de Ville and Notre Dame. The Municipal Palace—Handsome Building—Night—Illuminated—The Cathedral of Notre Dame—The Grandest and most interesting building in gay Paris—Interior—A procession moves across the scene.

PAINTED EXPRESSLY FOR THE PROPRIETOR BY M. DOUBELL AND COMPANY, THE

CRYPT OF THE HOLY SEPULCHRE.

[illegible] BEAUTIFUL CHANGES.

PIMLICO ROOMS,

WINCHESTER STREET, PIMLICO.

TUESDAY & WEDNESDAY,

MARCH 28th & 29th, 1865

[illegible] Drake will preside at a brilliant toned Organ Harmonium

M. BENEDETTO'S

GRAND MOVING

PANORAMA

OF A JOURNEY FROM

ENGLAND TO INDIA.

All the Effects are produced and the PANORAMA Illuminated by a NEW and POWERFUL APPARATUS, whose Brilliancy comprises one of the Eminently superior features of this Exhibition of Artistic Genius, scarcely surpassed by the ELECTRIC LIGHT, and capable of throwing A PICTURE ONE HUNDRED AND TWENTY FEET in circumference. The Paintings are the result of Long Years of Toil, Travel and Study, and such a GLORIOUS ARRAY of mental conception and skilful manipulation has never before been presented to a British audience. During the Evening the Lecturer will dilate upon the Adventures of

CAPTAIN SPEKE AND GRANT

AND THEIR WONDERFUL DISCOVERY OF THE

SOURCE OF THE NILE!

Incidentally also will be dwelt upon the Difficulties, Obstacles, and Probabilities of Success of the attempt to CONNECT the WATERS of the MEDITERRANEAN WITH RED SEA, by means of

SUEZ CANAL.

PROGRAMME.

ISLE OF WIGHT.. OSBORNE...London to Southampton—As the Curtain Rises the Vessel will be seen steaming from the Docks—Beautiful Scene—Grand Panoramic View of the Island—First Night at Sea—Passing the Needles—Moonlight.

STORM.. BAY OF BISCAY...Lightning—Flash upon Flash, Lighting up the Berlingas. Heavy Rolling Sea—The Gallant Ship seen struggling through the foam.

VIEW OF CINTRA...SUNSET...Deightful View of the Town from the Sea—Ruined Moorish Castles—La Penna The Palace.

TOWN OF TARIFA AND ROCK OF GIBRALTAR...The Mouldering Ramparts of Tarifa look as if it could be battered down with oranges.—Giant Fortifications.

CAPE TRAFALGAR & RIVER TAGUS. Corner of Europe and Africa—Battle of Trafalgar—Death of NELSON—"England expects every man to do his duty!"

SPLENDID VIEW OF ALGIERS..Capital of Algeria—Glorious View of the Old and New Town—Mosques and Marabouts—The CASBAN—Handsome Arcades—

VIEW OF MALTA & VALETTA—Sunset—Calm—Evening—Distant view of the Town—Fort Ricasoli—Panoramic View of the Great Harbour from the Upper Baracca

CITY OF ALEXANDRIA BY NIGHT—The Effects produced are truly beautiful.

JOURNEY UP THE MAHMOUDIE CANAL—Frightful sacrifice of 30,000 Lives.

PORT OF BOULAC—Night—Red glare of light illuminates the hurry and bustle of the sce[ne]

GRAND CAIRO—CEMETERY—SPLENDID TOMBS & CENTRAL STATION—These views are pronounced the most beautiful ever executed—The Last of the Mamelukes—The Funeral Procession—Religious Ideas—Crossing the Desert.

THE DEAD CAMEL...ARABS & MOORS—Touching Incident—Dangerous Gentry—NIGHT ENCAMPMENT—The Camp Fire—Preparing supper on the Isthmus of Sue[z] JOSEPH'S WELL—EGYPTIAN WOMEN—Peculiar modesty—Ladies of the Har[e]m

LEAVING SUEZ & DOWN THE RED SEA—The Hotel—Native Barber—The voyage JEDDAH, Port of MECCA—Graceful Arab Craft sailing down the shores of Arabia ROCK of ADEN—On the top of the highest peak the Meteor Flag of England is Flying POINT DE GALLE, CEYLON—Adam's Peak—Splendour of the Scenery.

The Second Portion of this Unique and Popular Entertainment consists of a Number of Beautiful Illustrations—Forming a Magnificent Dissolving

DIORAMA

GRAND MOVING VIEWS OF

MADRAS & CALCUTTA,

ENGLISH HOMES IN INDIA—1857.—First Suspicions of Treachery—A Work of Ar[t]

WOMEN & CHILDREN—A visit to the Well—Sepoy barbarity—Religious Ideas—

SCENE OF A GREAT TRAGEDY—Reminiscences of the past—Interior of the hous[e]

THE FUGITIVES—Melancholy mode of travelling—Lost to home and friends.

VIEW FROM A MINARET—Native Soldiers drunk with passion and plunder—

CITY OF DELHI—A Ride through the streets—Orange Groves and Splendid Building[s]

BUNGALOW IN FLAMES—Barbarous acts of the Mutineers—Horrors Ineffable.

ADVENTURE AT MEERUT—Attacked by hundreds of Sepoys—Moments of suspense

AN EMPEROR'S TOMB—The Grandeur of Ancient Eastern Architecture.

HANDSOME GATEWAY—Sunset, and splendid Eastern sky.—Camels and Elephant[s]

ATTACK OF THE HIGHLANDERS—A deadly struggle—Enemy in immense for[ce]

VIEW OF LUCKNOW—Striking Beauty of the Town.—Lucknow during the Seige.

HEROISM OF AN ENGLISH GIRL—Miss Wheeler defending herself from Rebels

THE JUDGMENT—Indiscriminate Executions.—Firing Mutineers from the Guns.

BEFORE CAWNPORE—Entering the deadly breach amid the rain of shot and shell.

"THE CAMPBELLS ARE COMING!"—Relief of Lucknow—The Highland Jessi[e]

THE CONCLUDING PORTION OF THIS CAPITAL EVENING'S ENTERTAINMENT CONSISTS OF A LARGE NUMBER OF AMUSING ENGLISH HISTORIC SKETCHES, THE GREATEST NOVELTY EVER WITNESSED.

Admission 1s Reserved 1s 6d Area 6[d]

Children under 12 and Schools Half-pri[ce]

Tickets may be had of Mr. ELGAR, Librarian.

Commence at EIGHT- Open Half-an-hour previous.

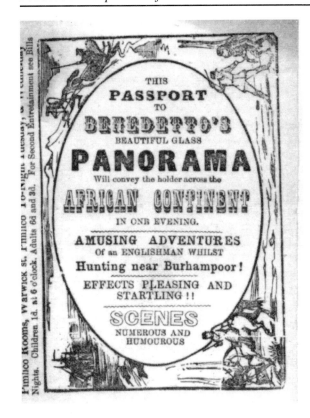

THIS PASSPORT TO BENEDETTO'S BEAUTIFUL GLASS PANORAMA Will convey the holder across the AFRICAN CONTINENT IN ONE EVENING. AMUSING ADVENTURES Of an ENGLISHMAN WHILST Hunting near Burhampoor! EFFECTS PLEASING AND STARTLING !! SCENES NUMEROUS AND HUMOUROUS

Pimlico Rooms, Warwick St., Pimlico 10-Night Tuesday, For Second Entertainment see Bills Nights. Children 1d. at 6 o'clock. Adults 6d and 3d.

when the bridge was opened, although the name of the 'White Ferry House' was, rather mysteriously, transferred to a new pub in Sutherland Street, quite a distance from the river.

For indoor entertainment, Pimlico residents could go to the Pimlico Rooms in Winchester Street, which opened in 1861. The building was constructed in the new Gothic style, of yellow brick banded with red and brown. This was the home of the Pimlico Literary, Scientific and Mechanics Institute, which moved here from Ebury Street. It was an appropriate spot for a district venue, next door to the famous Monster pub and on the site of the Neat House itself. The Rooms were considered to be 'of great utility and importance to the large locality of Pimlico'. Facilities included chess-rooms, class-rooms, a library and 'a convenient reading-room, furnishing means for rational amusement and improvement to the mind'.

Public gatherings of all kinds were indeed held here, from ratepayers' meetings to the soirees of the St George's Choral Society, but the emphasis on 'rational amusement' was interpreted somewhat broadly. Mr

Benedetto's panoramas were early favourites. In 1865, Pimlico was presented with 'a grand moving Panorama of a journey from England to India', and five years later with 'a colossal DIORAMA of the Mediterranean Coast and Continental Scenery'. Other entertainments included Miss Florence Lindgren 'in her new and startling Magical Illusion' (1865), and in 1875 the Royal Aboriginal Minstrels came to perform.

Although Pimlico was essentially a dormitory suburb for people working elsewhere, there was plenty of work available locally for its increasingly large working class population, and, unusually, for women in particular. Women were employed, 'with great advantage and propriety' at Colonel Colt's armoury in Bessborough Place, for the work required 'incessant attention rather than great strength'. Over 150 people were employed in conditions that must have been unusually good, for the factory won the praise of Charles Dickens. 'Having the fear of France before our eyes, we trust that the day will not be far distant when every Englishman, who can afford it, will be provided with his 'revolver' to meet any emergency', opined the Civil Service Gazette in 1853, but it was the fear of Russia that made the money for the Colonel's Pimlico operation. 25,540 revolvers were supplied by Colt's to the British Army during the Crimean War, and when the war had ended, and Colt's had moved away, the factory was taken over by the Army and became the Royal Small Arms Repair Establishment.

The Army seems to have rather liked Pimlico, for two years later, in 1859, the Royal Army Clothing Store moved into Cubitt's former workshops on Thames Bank. Described as 'one of the largest institutions that has ever been established for the organisation and utilisation of women's work', over a thousand women - 'what may be called the pick of the sewing-machine population of London' - were employed to make up military uniforms. The Clothing Store's products won little praise. One observer, who noted that

The Royal Army Clothing Store.

the cloth was cut in batches of twenty 'like fretwood', decided that it probably did not matter too much, since military training produced a standard size of man: 'a series of similar figures for which the sizes of the clothing factory are designed'.

The wharves and workshops of the riverbank provided much employment. Many were at first taken by firms involved in the building of Pimlico and Belgravia, and, like Cubitt's own works, found other uses once construction work was finished. Fabricotti's, by Vaux-

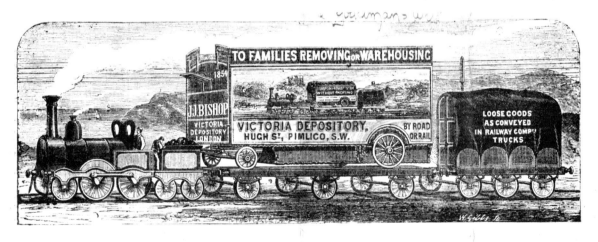

hall Bridge, eventually became the site of Hovis' principle flour mills and survived until well after the last war. The 1881 census reveals that Pimlico's riverside streets had a decidedly nautical flavour. Lightermen, merchant seamen, naval officers, ships' carpenters and sailors' wives all made their homes here, and an Argentine sea-captain had gone aground in Claverton Street. Coal merchants such as Radford's, which boasted 'a numerous fleet of sea-going boats and barges', shared the Grosvenor Road wharves with more specialist firms such as Broadwood's, world-famous piano-makers. Their woodyard, on the site of Crown Reach, was piled high with quality timber from every corner of the world - 'from the dense backwoods of the wild west to the stately historical wealds of England'. Baltic Wharf, by Vauxhall Bridge, belonged to a shipbreaking firm who adorned their premises with figureheads from old naval battleships, 'looking with solemnity over the wall'.

St Gabriel's, Warwick Square.

A Possible Place for a Pope ?

Pimlico was well endowed with churches, which were seen as lending focus and respectability to a neighbourhood. Two of the three squares were thus blessed. St Gabriel's, the first, presides over Warwick Square. Designed by the Grosvenor Estate surveyor, Thomas Cundy, and consecrated in 1853, St Gabriel's became effectively the parish church of Pimlico. Its congregation built and ran a primary school as well as a working men's institute, and later did what they could to ameliorate the conditions of Pimlico's increasingly poor population. St Saviour's in St George's Square, also designed by Cundy, was not built until 1864, when the Square had already been laid out. More churches were built on the fringes of Pimlico. The foundation stone for Holy Trinity, in Bessborough Gardens, was laid in 1849; the church was the gift of a very wealthy Archdeacon of Westminster. It has since been demolished, but for long acted as an attractive landmark for people approaching the city over Vauxhall Bridge.

There were several chapels catering for nonconformists: a Wesleyan chapel in Claverton Street, and the Eccleston Square Congregational Chapel in Belgrave Road, which opened in 1848 and was described as 'peculiarly adapted to the genteel neighbourhood in which it now stands'. Less genteel churchgoers were catered for in separate buildings, to avoid the mutual embarrassment (for so it was perceived) of all classes sharing the same place of worship. All Saints 'iron church' in Grosvenor Road, next door to Johnson's Thames Parade, was opened in 1860: it was rebuilt in 1871, and demolished in the 1970s. St John's, Wilton Road, a daughter church of St Peter's in Eaton Square, was consecrated in 1874; it too is no more, having been destroyed by a direct hit during the bombing of 1940. St James the Less, built in 1858-61, served the poorer streets around Vauxhall Bridge Road: the *Illustrated London News* said that it rose 'as a lily among weeds'. Designed by G E Street, architect of the Law Courts, it has been described as 'one of the

most original and remarkable churches in London'.

St Barnabas', in Pimlico Road, opened its doors in June 1850, following an appeal by the Revd William Bennett to his Belgravian parishioners for funds to build a church that would serve 'a population of poor men, women and children, striving labouring men working from hand to mouth to sustain life'. Bennett, however, was no ordinary evangelist. He was a follower of Edward Pusey, one of the founders of the Oxford Movement and all that is today considered to be 'High Church'. Bennett and Pusey shared a grand mission: 'to rechristianise the heathen masses of a Christian country'. They hoped to lure the heathen back by reintroducing colour and ritual into the somewhat austere and frugal mid-century Church; but on the eve of the Great Exhibition, when Britain was seen

as 'the Workshop of the World', 'Puseyism' to many seemed like a great leap backwards.

Public opinion rumbled, and to cap it all the Pope chose that particular time to create a dozen new English Roman Catholic bishoprics. There was an uproar, and immediately people began to accuse Bennett and Pusey of paving the way for a Catholic takeover. The little church in Pimlico Road suddenly became a centre of national controversy. 'For days and days there was not a single newspaper but teemed with letters and articles about our poor inoffensive Church', lamented the vicar. *Punch* even suggested that if the Pope were forced to quit Rome 'he will emigrate to Pimlico, and make Belgravia the future residence of the Popes'.

Large-scale rioting took place at St Barnabas'

UNABRIDGED EDITION.—WITH ALL THE OMITTED PASSAGES.

ASTOUNDING REVELATIONS
OF

PUSEYISM IN BELGRAVIA,

CONTAINING THE MOST FRIGHTFUL DISCLOSURES OF DIABOLICAL
PLOTS AGAINST FEMALE CHASTITY BY THE

REV. MR. POOLE AND MISS JOY,
AT

THE FASHIONABLE CHURCH OF ST. BARNABAS, PIMLICO.

Showing the temptations held out by the Confessional to entrap innocent Girls,
virtuous Wives, and helpless Widows, to minister to the lascivious desires of Romish
Priests in the guise of Protestant Clergymen; with Descriptive Particulars of the
fearful Chamber of Private Inquisition, where the most disgusting and abominable
practices were carried on, as detailed by the

HON. AND REV. F. BARING,

At the Great Public Meeting held in St. James's Hall, Piccadilly, on Friday, June 11,
1858, together with the Bishop of London's Decision on the facts, all of which were
revealed in the presence of a vast Assembly of Three Thousand Persons, among whom
were Two Hundred and Fifty Members of Parliament and Peers.

PRICE ONE PENNY.

LONDON: J. HATSWELL, 8, BROADWAY, LUDGATE-HILL.

'Lilley's Corner', a bustling store on the edge of Cubitt's Pimlico.

during November and December 1850, both in the surrounding streets and inside the church itself during Sunday services. 'A very large mob of most tumultuous and disorderly persons' besieged the church. One hundred policemen had to be drafted in to keep control. St Barnabas' was rapidly becoming an embarrassment to the church authorities, and in March 1851 Dr Blomfield, the Bishop of London, gladly accepted the Revd Bennett's resignation: it is somewhat ironic that it should be the bishop, and not the vicar, whose name is commemorated in Blomfield Terrace, the street that runs beside the church.

The disorders died down after Bennett's departure, but St Barnabas' retained its notoriety. In 1858 the church was the subject of a remarkable pamphlet, which claimed to reveal 'the most frightful disclosures of diabolical plots against female chastity ... showing the temptation held out by the confessional to entrap innocent Girls, virtuous Wives and helpless Widows, to minister to the lascivious desires of Romish priests in the disguise of Protestant clergymen; with

Descriptive Particulars of the fearful Chamber of Private Inquisition, where the most disgusting and abominable practices were carried on'. The revelations did not live up to the promise of the title, however; there was no repeat of 1851, and the little church in Pimlico Road remained steadfastly 'High'. It was the rest of the country that changed, and by 1900 the ritual and pageantry pioneered at St Barnabas' was found in churches throughout the land. St Barnabas' itself became very fashionable, and its services were attended by such distinguished local residents as Aubrey Beardsley, who lived in Cambridge Street. Described by Sir John Betjeman as 'a jewel of a church', the peaceful precinct of St Barnabas' today is one of the district's greatest attractions.

Shops and Schools

Cubitt had been careful to ensure that shops did not impair the value of his development. Restrictions were placed on such 'offensive trades' as baking or fish-selling, and the main

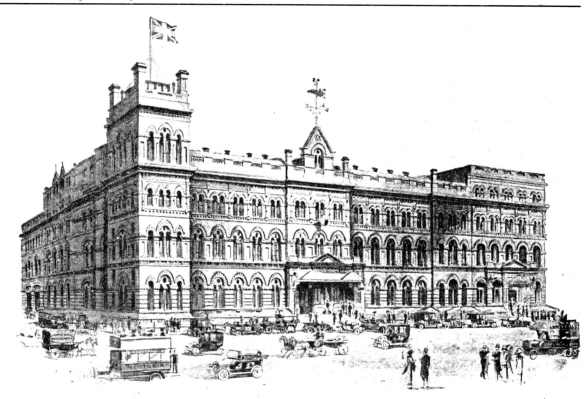

Army and Navy stores, Victoria Street, in 1914

shopping areas were confined to Pimlico's periphery - Lupus Street, near the wharves and warehouses of the riverside, and at the eastern end of Warwick Way (then called Warwick Street). Small clusters of shops only were permitted in the central, 'posher' area, for instance in Cambridge and Sussex Streets: a pattern that has remained unchanged.

The wealthier inhabitants were expected to send out for their shopping, and later chose to patronise the new department stores along Buckingham Palace Road and Victoria Street. 'The rich buy at the Army and Navy stores', wrote Booth bluntly in 1898. Pimlico nonetheless had a surprising range of specialist suppliers. 'Lupus Street is great in shops - a suburban Bond Street or High Street or Cheapside, a little of the best of each', enthused 'W M A', that great if mysterious fan of Pimlico, in 1877; and indeed, the street's retailers that year included four artists' colourmen, a piano maker, an embroiderer, a professor of dancing, and even a photographer.

Street-markets were certainly not on Cubitt's

agenda. Indeed, leases granted to shops included the specific requirement that shopfronts had to be properly glazed, as open shop-fronts might lower the tone of the area, but in fact the stalls began to appear almost as soon as Pimlico was built. A well-established street-market across the tracks in Pimlico Road was soon competing with stalls in Moreton Street, Churton Street and Lupus Street, whose 'lively line of barrows' survived until the Churchill Gardens Estate was built in the 1950s. Pimlico's biggest street market was in Warwick Way, and extended from Belgrave Road to Vauxhall Bridge Road. It began in the late 1860s: 'Warwick Street has gone into the stalls of the sake of hoisery and vegetables', lamented one resident - 'commercial and a trifle vulgar, but still successful'. Local residents considered it 'objectionable', and tried to have it closed down, but the authorities, petitioned by the Warwick Way shopkeepers, allowed it to remain. By 1893, the Warwick Street market had become the largest in the area. Its 63 traders included two toy-dealers and no less than seventeen flower sellers, and the market survived until 1945, when it was moved

St Michael's schools in 1848.

around the corner into Tachbrook Street.

Children are unruly, and schools, like shops, were considered to lower the tone. The children of Pimlico's more prosperous residents went to schools elsewhere, and at first

Cubitt made no provision for the rest. Not until 1848 was the first school built. St Michael's School had places for 125 boys and 125 girls, strictly segregated, and 140 infants. It was situated right on the edge of Pimlico, on the banks of the canal itself, and

Wesleyan Chapel in Claverton Street.

51

Colonel Colt's controversial armoury; the rooftop lettering is clearly visible.

the public were reassured that the children's entrances were on the canal side 'so that the occupiers of the houses in Hugh-street will not be subjected to noise'. The building was demolished when the railway came, and the school moved to Buckingham Palace Road.

Other basic education was provided by the churches. The Wesleyans ran a small infants school, and in 1853 St Gabriel's Church began to hold classes 'in a miserable hired room'. A public meeting, held in 1861, decided that 'the rapid increase in the number

In the wilderness of Southern Pimlico. Warwick Square in 1907.

'The West End Railway District', from the Illustrated London News, *9 April 1859. A fascinating and surprisingly accurate panorama of Cubitt's Pimlico. The piers for the new railway bridge are being constructed, but the Grosvenor Canal still looks bright and busy.*

of the poorer classes in this district renders it a matter of urgent necessity to provide means for the education of their children', and within a year the Church had opened a primary school on Distillery Lane (later Glasgow Terrace), under the lee of Octavius Smith's establishment. St Gabriel's school was very popular, and some were soon complaining of the classrooms' 'crowded state'. In 1871, the Wesleyan Methodists opened the Pimlico Day School in part of the Pimlico Rooms; here, for sixpence a week, children over seven could gain a basic education. Infants were half price.

Respectable, if Dull

'Such was Belgravia once - a waste unknown! Behold that desert now - a generous town!', enthused an early resident of London's most successful development. Thomas Cubitt's famous mansions not only found buyers

with remarkable speed, but buyers who were officially described as 'the richest population in the world'. Even the capital's first skyscrapers at the Albert Gate, nicknamed Malta and Gibraltar 'because no-one could ever take them', soon found occupants. One of them was taken by the French, whose embassy remains there to this day.

Cubitt's contemporaries anticipated similar things for Pimlico, which, the Builder declared in 1845, 'from being heretofore little better than a swamp, perfectly valueless and most injurious to the health of the neighbourhood, now promises to become one of the most splendid and luxurious quarters of the neighbourhood'. Cubitt certainly went to great lengths to ensure the social cachet of his new district. He was proud of the fact that his 'plan has been to allow fewer public houses than is generally done by other Builders', and, as we have seen, his leases were carefully drawn up to ensure that 'offensive'

occupations were zoned onto particular streets.

His monopoly south of the canal gave him the power to exclude undesirable new development. In 1835, Cubitt took an eight-acre site next to the canal chiefly to prevent its being developed for industrial use, and the appearance of wharves along both the canal and the river was strictly controlled; along the canal, they were augmented with railings and shrubberies: curtain walls and a screen of trees concealed the riverside wharves from passers-by. Cubitt could do less about existing development. White's timber-yard, on the site of the modern Tachbrook Estate between Lupus Street and the river, was sold to the Equitable Gas-works company, whose establishment 'W M A' considered to be the 'bete noire' of Pimlico. Cubitt did his best to make life difficult for Octavius Smith's distillery, for instance by refusing permission to use St George's Drive for distillery traffic while Ebury Bridge was being rebuilt. The small pocket of ill-built cottages and slums around Garden Row was effectively screened from the more prosperous parts of Pimlico by Lillington Street, abandoned to shops and commerce since, as Cubitt later told the landlords, 'we had great fear of the success'.

Cubitt had more problems with the Crown-owned land around Vauxhall Bridge, which had been leased in 1825 to a much less astute developer than himself. Part of it was let, as a local remembered, to 'an eccentric old gentleman, one Andrew Mann, [who] had every here and there, on either side of the road, a strange accumulation of huge pieces of old ironware, principally tubing, which it delighted the street boys of that day to crawl through ... on the Pimlico side was a huge pile of old earthenware brown and yellow pie dishes piled against the back wall of an old house and numbering at least some thousands'.

In 1838 Cubitt took over the lease, demolished the buildings already erected, and promptly screened the Equitable Gasworks

from the rest of Pimlico by building a four-storey workshop, three hundred feet long, which in 1844 he returned to the Government for use as workshops while the new Houses of Parliament were being built. The job completed, however, the Government leased the building to Colonel Colt, much to Cubitt's horror. 'The colonel has resently been having his siyn painted on the roof of the shop which causes considerable attention [sic]', wrote an employee in 1853. 'It is one hundred and seventy-six feet in length with ... fourteen foot letters, 'Colonel Colt's Patent Firearms Manufactory' in the wording ... for the first few days that it was up there was a crowed to be seen at all hours of the day viewing it'. Cubitt used his influence to get the sign removed, but the small-arms factory itself remained. Industry - Colt's enterprise, the distillery and the gasworks, Cubitt's own factory - doomed the social success of southern Pimlico. Although the bridegroom in Anthony Trollope's 1864 novel *The Small House at Allington* wanted to buy a house in 'one of the new Pimlico squares down near Vauxhall Bridge and the river', a socially-astute friend of the bride strongly advised against it: 'For heaven's sake, my dear, don't let him take you anywhere beyond Eccleston Square'.

William Gaspey in 1851 decribed Cubitt's Pimlico houses as 'respectable if dull ... suitable to the rather unfashionable clientele for which it seems to have been created'. Outside the main squares and thoroughfares, clerks and well-to-do tradesmen shared streets with lodging-houses of greater or lesser respectability. In Cambridge Street in 1851, they included messengers, travelling salesmen and a variety of clerks: the upwardly-mobile of their day. Gaspey summed up Cubitt's Pimlico as 'less recherche than the north side of Belgravia, but perfectly well suitable on its own terms'. To the inhabitants of humble Battersea, Pimlico in 1858 still seemed to be 'the ultra-genteel district', but any hopes that Pimlico might have become a second Belgravia were finally dashed in 1860, when the railway came to Victoria.

6 Shabby Gentility and Vice

'The New Victoria Railway Station at Pimlico', 1861.

Victoria

Victoria Station is named after Victoria Street, begun in 1844. Broad, straight, strident, the new highway cut right through the crooked alleys, slums and rookeries of old Westminster, and the Victorians were very proud of it. 'One of the sights of London', a journalist declared at the opening. Victoria Street joined the old Chelsea road (Buckingham Palace Road) just at the head of the Grosvenor Basin. It was an ideal position for a major railway terminus - a fact that was not lost on one enterprising railway company, which in 1858 brought their tracks to a temporary terminus across the river, near the site of Battersea Power Station, and cheekily called it 'Pimlico'.

Trade on the Grosvenor Canal had dropped off significantly once the building of Belgravia and Pimlico was complete. In 1858, a protagonist for the new railway described it as being in 'a state of desuetude', and two of the canal's major wharfingers, Jackson and Kelk, were among the entrepreneurs who formed

the Victoria Station and Pimlico Railway Company. The Company promoted a private Bill in Parliament to get the station built.

It was bitterly opposed in the House of Commons. Despite the promises of a *Times* columnist that the new station would 'purge and cleanse the dirty parts of Pimlico', the locals were not convinced. Although the days of the Ranelagh Gardens and the waterside walkways were long gone, the canal still had some amenity value. Wealthy Pimlico pioneers such as the Revd James Hammond, and the society artist James Swinton, chose to build themselves substantial houses on its banks: Swinton, whose house on St George's Drive had a 126-foot frontage to the canal, had tried (unsuccessfully) to get permission to open gates onto the towpath.

Railways, on the other hand, were disastrous to the success of a prestigious development such as Pimlico, as Cubitt knew very well. In 1834 the Great Western Railway had hoped

to build a terminus near Vauxhall Bridge, which would have involved bringing the railway across modern Pimlico from Lower Sloane Street, but Cubitt immediately objected, and the railway company chose Paddington instead. Other plans - to build a terminus on Lupus Street, or Horseferry Road, were similarly rejected out of hand. But Cubitt had died in 1855: had he still been alive, Victoria Station might never have been built. The Act was passed in August 1858, but not before some major concessions had been wrung from the promoters. Ebury Bridge was to be widened to sixty feet and the other bridges rebuilt - with 'parapets of handsome elevation, Eight Feet high at least', adorned with ornamental shrubs which the railway company was obliged to keep 'in good, substantial and ornamental Order and Repair'.

All building work had to be submitted to the Grosvenor Estate for approval, which retained the right to first refusal on the sale of any superfluous land - an important measure that helped Pimlico to retain its architectural unity. The railway had to be roofed in from the station right down to the end of Alderney Street, and the same section of rail had to be laid 'on longitudinal sleepers, bedded in elastic material so as to be as noiseless as possible'. Such restrictions certainly added considerably to the cost, but the railway company had nonetheless got a bargain: a truly central London terminus, involving virtually no demolition work and the costly compensation that went with it. The station was opened quietly in October 1860 without any ceremony - 'the doors were thrown open, passengers took their tickets and the trains started as though the line had been in working order for years'.

Inexpressible Vice and Debauchery

The Grosvenor Hotel, with its distinctive Prussian-spiked roofs, was built to screen the station from Belgravian eyes, but from Wilton Road and Pimlico the view was strictly utilitarian. It was symbolic, for the arrival of Victoria ended Pimlico's social aspirations overnight. The railway itself ran like a scar around Pimlico; leafy Streatham and Brixton suddenly came within easy commuting dis-

St. George's Square and Belgrave Road, S.W.1.

Police vigilance on Belgrave Road, c 1900.

The Wilton Hotel, in Wilton Road, had quite a reputation for 'iniquitous business'.

tance, and Central London abruptly ceased to be the place to be. Pimlico soon became a sort of annexe to the station, its larger houses transformed into hotels, boarding-houses and other, seedier, establishments catering for the varied needs of the capital.

Almost immediately, prostitution became endemic. As early as 1863, a Claverton Street resident was complaining that brothels were leading to 'the rapidly increasing demolition of Pimlico'; a ratepayers' group counted 180 of them. Three years later, Turpentine Lane was described as 'the nightly scene of inexpressible vice and debauchery'. The Grosvenor Estate eventually appointed a

Moreton Place, c 1900.

plain-clothes detective to spy out prostitutes, but his success was limited. He was replaced by a uniformed Beadle, whose duty it was to patrol the streets for eight hours a day, and inform the curious that he was employed 'to preserve the respectability of the neighbourhood', but he too was unable to stem the tide, and was removed in 1883.

A flurry of residents' groups appeared in reaction to the problem: the St George's Vigilance Society, the Association for the Suppression of Disorderly Houses in South Belgravia, and the Pimlico Ratepayers' Defence Association. A petition was presented to the Vestry in 1882, signed by 100 'respectable striving people ... brought to the last stages of poverty through their inability to let their apartments'. John Lane, secretary of the PRDA, believed that prostitution kept rent levels abnormally high: 'the fictitious rents which have sprung up frequently deter honest people from taking the homes', he told the *Westminster and Pimlico News*. Lane cited the example of a brothel in Sussex Street whose proprietor charged her tenants a guinea a bottle for brandy:

'what respectable lodging-house keeper could compete with a person carrying on an iniquitous business like that?'

For many boarding-house proprietors, the only option was to turn to brothel-keeping themselves. The process was neatly summed up in a court case fifty years later: 'A woman decides to take on an 'apartment house' in Pimlico, but she had no business experience, and she was not fitted to run such a house in a neighbourhood like Pimlico. She could not give the tenants the service they had been used to in the past, and the next stage was a house empty of tenants. Then women of certain characters came to the house and rented rooms'. The residents' associations had some short-term success in bringing prosecutions against brothel-keepers, but they failed in their attempts to reverse 'the growing notoriety of the neighbourhood'. Charles Booth described the district as 'an admixture of shabby gentility and vice'. In some streets, one house in three was said to be a brothel, and the streets were 'swarming with prostitutes'. Prostitution continued to contribute to the Pimlico economy until recent times.

Lupus Street in 1905.

The Migration of Fashion

Pimlico ratepayers were convinced that it was the brothels 'which deterred respectable people from coming to live here', but there were other and more obvious forces at work. Booth called it 'the migration of fashion from Pimlico'. A local churchman, describing Tachbrook Street in the 1890s, noted that it had been 'for many years occupied by well-to-do 'city men', who gradually forsook it as the facilities for locomotion enabled them to migrate to the suburbs. Many of the houses are now let in apartments to the working classes'. Many of them had never been inhabited by 'well-to-do city men' at all. Cubitt, like most developers, built his houses as large as he dared - and as a result many of

St Saviour's Church, St. George's Square. S. W.

St George's Square in 1910.

them stayed empty for years. The Grosvenor Estate's advisers had urged him to be less ambitious, and noted that he had a reputation for it: in Bloomsbury, Cubitt was said to have regretted building houses that 'were rather too large, and too expensive, for the locality'.

New developments elsewhere in London were continually dispossessing poorer people, who came in ever greater numbers to places like Pimlico, where the houses were hard to let. Already by 1861 there was much middle-class concern at 'the rapid increase in the number of the poorer classes in this district'; in 1894, the problems of the area were held to include 'the variety and constant change of the people; the poverty and dissolute habits of many ... and the constant pouring in ... of poor and starving people, often bringing with them the fevers and other diseases, and causing much misery to those whose misfortune it was to live near them'.

The earliest attempts to provide decent housing specifically for Pimlico's poorer residents came in 1876, when the first blocks in Peabody Avenue were opened on land that had once belonged to the Waterworks Company and the railway. For most, however, there was little alternative but to take a room, or part of a room, in one of Cubitt's houses. 'Houses originally built for small middle class families have become turned into what I may not unfairly call 'rookeries' for the poor', observed the Vicar of St Gabriel's in 1891. 'There are several streets of houses which look from the outside the prosperous homes of middle class folk, but are let out in tenements, 4 or 5 families in each house', his successor wrote a few years later, 'in some houses each room being tenanted by a distinct family'. The owners of these properties were not usually rack-renters or profiteers, but small investors who may have sunk 'their whole life's savings in properly furnishing and equipping a house to be let out as good-class lodgings', as a sympathiser pointed out. They had as much interest as anyone in maintaining at least the veneer of prosperity - but rarely the resources to do so.

Part of the problem lay with the imposing stucco facades that are so characteristic of Pimlico, but which are so costly to maintain. Already by 1858 people were complaining about the 'ugly stucco exteriors which have to be painted every two or three years'. Westmoreland Terrace was said to be 'looking as if clad in perennial drab' little more than ten years after it was built. Pimlico's drabness made a big impression on Charles Booth: 'at best it is a depressing district, passing ... from the shabbiness of shabby gentility to the gradual decay and grimy dilapidation which is apt to overtake houses built for another class, and altogether unsuited for their present occupants; short of paint, the plaster peeling and cracking; sordid and degraded dwellings, they remain a nightmare in the memory'.

A Retired Suburb

Booth's was an extreme view, of course, and by no means shared by all Pimlico's residents. 'There is no more desirable quarter of London in my opinion', said John Lane in 1887. It was central, accessible, healthy, and 'the houses, too, are almost all well built and roomy'. The sadly anonymous, but delightfully partisan 'W.M.A.', who made his or her observations on 'Stuccoville' in 1877, had no doubts about the district's cachet: 'South Belgravia is genteel, sacred to professional men of various grades, not rich enough to luxuriate in Belgravia proper, but rich enough to live in private homes - for this is a retired suburb. Here people are more lively than in Kensington, though not so grand, of course, as in Albertopolis, and yet a cut above Chelsea, which is only commercial ... the genteel

part lies in a small space, the immediate neighbourhood of Gloucester, Sussex, Cambridge, Sutherland Streets - while Lupus Street is the sweet south that borders this paradise of rest. This is the abode of gentility - a servant or two in the kitchen, birds in the windows, with flowers in boxes, pianos, and the latest fashions, of course'.

Booth conceded that Pimlico still retained an attraction for the disreputable wealthy - 'rich vagrants and bachelors, and Members of Parliament'. And even he had to admit that 'there is an absence of marked poverty, and every indication throughout of working or middle class comfort, and of what aims at fashion and may pass for wealth in the squares and principal streets': he singled out St George's Square, which he said 'has an out of the way charm of its own which, making little pretence after fashion, seems to defy decay'.

In Pimlico, Booth learnt, 'people are not to be accounted poor, and some of them, we are told, resented the introduction of a curate because he came from the East End and therefore should not be a suitable man for them'. The Conservative vote was, in 1910, said to possess 'an overwhelming preponderance. In Pimlico, the one-sidedness of the constituency renders organisation almost unnecessary'. Their candidate, naturally, won both 1910 elections with large majorities. Suffragettes picketting Pimlico's polling stations 'did not succeed in gaining many signatures', and the defeated Liberal candidate declared 'unhesitatingly that here in Pimlico if a tradesman dared to show a Radical flag or poster he was boycotted'.

For Pimlico, on the eve of World War One, still saw itself as an eminently genteel neighbourhood. For sixty pounds a year, 'a superior quiet family - no children' could rent a house in Moreton Street. Pimlico's daughters could take dancing lessons at one of half-a-dozen local schools, and for ten-and-six a month Papa could buy a piano from Dove's of Pimlico Road to grace the drawing-room. Adventurous residents went to find amusement around the station. Wilton Road, which the *Daily Telegraph* in 1908 called 'that great home of the Italian cafe', was also the home of London's first cinema, the Bioscope, opened in 1905 by an American called Washington Grant.

Opposite the terminus stood the Royal Standard Music Hall, one of London's oldest. The Standard offered up to twenty acts a night. The Easter Monday programme in 1910 featured Baby Vi Davis, the Three Orleans, Benn's Dutch Boys and Girls; film clips of the boat race and the Grand National, and two 'capital sketches' - 'Our Mary Jane, a side-splitting servant story', and 'Olga's Oath', a dramatic presentment of Nihilist life in Russia'. It was the Standard's boast that they supplied 'wholesome entertainment at charges within reach of all', and the proprietor was said to have 'won countless friends in Westminster and Pimlico', but their range of entertainment was fast becoming dated. Not even the 'graphic Edisonograph living pictures' of its 1910 Whitsun programme could hold the audience, and that autumn the Standard closed its doors: the Victoria Palace opened on the same site a year later.

Octavius Smith's Thames Bank Distillery finally closed in 1907, when nearly a hundred men were laid off. A year later, a group of local residents petitioned the Grosvenor Estate for permission to open 'a miniature rifle range' on the site. They did not succeed, but their intention shows the increasing militarism of the age. In 1910, the local MP campaigned successfully on the memorable slogan 'we only care for England, and the Empire; and we know that we are not safe'. Four years later, England was at war.

7 Pimlico Between the Wars

Women at work in Clarendon Street, 1918.

Appalling Overcrowding

'Once upon a time Pimlico, like Paradise, was a fair place, intersected with streams', wrote Ethel Woolmer in 1922. In 1922 that must have seemed like a very long time ago. Pimlico was one of several parts of London to suffer bomb damage during the First World

The north side of Vincent Street in 1928.

The south side of Vincent Street in 1928.

War. There were a number of air raids during 1917, and in October several houses in Glamorgan Street and Lupus Street were demolished or damaged; four people died. 'Lots of motors go about driven by coal gas, with great balloons full of this gas on top of them', wrote a Pimlico schoolboy to his cousin that year. 'Also you often see long queus [sic] of women waiting for their butter or sugar or tea rations ... on the day I come to London we have an air-raid, and we all bundled down into the cellar, at least it was the pantry really, and had dinner there'.

When the war was over, soldiers returning home were promised 'a land fit for heroes to live in' by Prime Minister Lloyd George. 'Homes fit for heroes', interpreted the papers, and the right to decent housing became the battle-cry of the 1920s. Overcrowding was a major problem, and particularly in places such as Pimlico. In 1919, the London Housing Board began to convert houses into flats along St George's Drive, Belgrave Road and elsewhere. That year the City Council

considered building 'blocks of tenement dwellings say four or five storeys in height'. Plans were soon launched to build the flats in Pimlico Road; Walden House, the first block, was opened in 1924. There were forty flats: the Council received twenty-five applications for each one. 'The terrible lack of good housing ... stares one in the face at every turn', reported a 1925 inquiry into the condition of Westminster's children; resulting in 'the twin evils for childhood of bad and dilapidated homes and of appalling overcrowding'.

Conditions south of Lupus Street were particularly bad. 'The poorest streets in Westminster are in the south of the Pimlico district near the river', a survey conducted by the London School of Economics reported in 1928. 'There is considerable poverty and overcrowding in Pulford Street and Aylesford Street'. That year the river burst its banks, and the scale of Pimlico's housing problem became national news.

The Year of the Floods

'The wall seemed to be blown into the air with a dull thud like a muffled shell bursting', said an eye-witness of the disastrous flood at Grosvenor Road (now Millbank) in 1928, when the Thames burst through its Pimlico parapets. 'The water came away like a mountain fall'.

John Johnson's development, by modern Claverton Street, was flooded a century earlier in 1827. Even when the Embankment had been built, in the 1850s, this stretch of river was regularly flooded. One reason for this was the removal of old London Bridge, whose many narrow arches had acted as a weir and so prevented the full force of the flood tides from surging beyond; old Westminster Bridge, its foundations weakened by the tides, was an early casualty. Committees sat, reports were made, and finally the parapets were raised - but not before 'the tremendous storm of wind and rain' of October 1882, which lifted Charing Cross Pier off its moorings, had managed to breach the feeble defences at the foot of St George's Square.

Pimlico was spared any major floods until 1928, however. On the night of January 7/8, the river rose level with the top of the parapet along Chelsea Embankment, and flooded three of old Chelsea Bridge's lodges. They had just been newly painted, as the LCC mournfully observed. The Army Clothing Store lost nearly 200,000 yards of khaki serge, flannel and cotton. Real disaster struck just below Vauxhall Bridge, where the parapet wall was breached in three places. In a matter of seconds the whole area south of Vincent Square was under water. 'Men struggled waist-deep in water, heroically trying to pull away iron bars surrounding basement windows already under water', wrote a journalist who was on the spot.

Page Street in 1931. The new flats are on the left.

THE EBURY BRIDGE HOUSING ESTATE.

The dwellings upon this Estate, developed by the Westminster City Council, stand where formerly ran the Canal of the Chelsea Waterworks made in 1724.

1731

1931

The Estate was formally opened on the 3rd November, 1931, by the Mayoress of the City of Westminster (Mrs. J. F. C. Bennett).

The first Tenant of Flat No.   in

House is Mr.

Mayor

Ten people drowned that night, despite the efforts of the emergency services. Hundreds of flats and houses were evacuated, many families camping out in local schools for weeks afterwards. The Tate's lower galleries were flooded, causing considerable damage to its collections. Animals suffered too: the death-toll included two goats, which had somehow ended up in the urban streets of Pimlico. Only the fish were pleased. Some found their way to the Grosvenor Hotel at Victoria; others turned up, conveniently enough, in the kitchen of Battersea Police Station. The Mayor of Westminster set up an emergency relief fund for the victims, and despite criticism that it took too long to pay out - 'sympathy without relief is like mustard without beef', in a critic's memorable phrase - the fund raised over £30,000, no mean sum in the 1920s.

The inquest on those drowned returned a verdict of accidental death, and absolved everybody from blame; but the tragedy on Grosvenor Road brought the plight of Pimlico's seven thousand basement dwellers to national attention. Amongst the first to lambast the authorities for their inaction were the members of the Fellowship Guild. This remarkable institution was based at the Guildhouse in Belgrave Road, once the Eccleston Square Chapel. The leading light was Dr Maude Royden, a Church of England preacher, once a prominent suffragette, and under her guidance the Guildhouse became an early focus for the women's movement: the Women Citizens Society held their meetings here throughout the 1930s. The Guildhouse was a centre for the League of Nations Union and for the League of Arts, and its members were outspoken on local matters of all kinds. In 1928 its members heartily endorsed the call from the Bishop of London for a major rebuilding programme. 'There are large numbers of 'homes', so-called, in and near Pimlico, which will never repay reconditioning. They should go, and go quickly', the Westminster Survey Group told the *Daily Telegraph*.

In 1929, the City Council began work on the Ebury Bridge estate; 220 flats were opened there in 1931, built on land reclaimed from the canal. Seventy-five cottages near Wilton

The Tachbrook Estate under construction.

Road 'in an advanced state of decay' were demolished: a move which, the Council declared, had 'entirely revolutionised the appearance of this area'. New flats were built at Page Street too, and by 1934 they felt able to say that Pimlico had 'greatly improved, thanks to the demolition of various old properties and the erection of ... more attractive buildings upon modern and progressive lines'.

In July 1935, the Westminster Housing Association opened the first blocks of the Tachbrook Estate, behind St George's Square; 180 flats were opened, housing 800 people. To its tenants, the brand-new estate must have seemed the height of luxury: the Trust claimed that they were 'the first working-class flats in London to be served by self-operational electric lifts'. The Association that year claimed that 'large numbers are still living in basements and in cramped lodgings which are ill provided with any of the decencies or amenities a civilised family should have', but it was not a view shared by the Council. 'No less than 56% [of tenanted houses] have baths and in only 25% can it be said that water supply is not readily available

to every tenant', declared the Medical Officer of Health with apparent satisfaction. Overcrowding in Pimlico eased as the thirties progressed. By 1938, only 622 families were still classed as living in crowded conditions, and that year the Council felt proud enough of its achievements to take the Queen Mother (Queen Mary) on a tour of its various housing schemes.

A Reasonably-Priced Lodging

Of Pimlico's 3,000 houses in 1935, only 846 were still occupied by single families. Most of the rest had long since been converted into boarding-houses of varying quality, for Pimlico had become the land of the lodger. 'You might try Pimlico', a room-hunting character was told in Gavin Douglas' novel *A Tale of Pimlico*; 'There's plenty of boarding-houses along St George's Road and up that way'. He noticed that 'most of the houses were shabby, some even dilapidated, and with paper taking the place of window-glass; but I was seeking no grandeur: only a

The original site of Victoria Coach Station in Lupus Street.

reasonably-priced lodging' - and sure enough, 'the third house I passed had a ticket showing Apartments to Let'. He took 'a large room with high ceiling and french windows facing the street. There was an iron-balustraded veranda outside the windows. A carved marble mantlepiece showed the room had been the principal drawing-room in the days when Pimlico was Society'.

Douglas' hero was paying thirty shillings a week for his room, but it was in St George's Drive. In 1939, a three-room unfurnished flat in Denbigh Street would have cost him 22s 6d weekly, or a top-floor flat in Ranelagh Road, 'large rooms, newly decorated' for 19s 6d. (By way of comparison, the wage of a City Council foreman painter that year was 84s per week; a 'third-division clerk' was paid £175 10s per year, or just over 63s per week). The advert also claimed that Ranelagh Road was 'a good address' - testimony to the sense of gentility that Pimlico, in spite of everything, still managed to retain. The Royal

Army Clothing Store was closed in 1933 because, as the local MP told his critics, it would have been 'criminal folly' to retain a factory 'in such a valuable situation'. In 1937, a development of 2,000 luxury flats was opened in its place, complete with its own shopping concourse, restaurant, swimming pool and ballroom.

This was Dolphin Square, the largest block of flats in Europe. The writer A P Herbert, commissioned to write the publicity brochure, began with the remarkable admission that he was too old-fashioned to appreciate the new development. 'I shall never, I think, dwell in the Dolphin City. For this, I have no doubt, is the dwelling of the future'. He did concede that the new development 'seems to be interesting, imaginative, bold and new'. His one concern was that the new occupants would be too pampered: 'these fortunate wives will not have enough to do', he wrote. 'A little drudgery is good for wives, perhaps. The Dolphin lady may be spoilt'.

Cement of the Empire

The architecture of Dolphin Square has evoked somewhat mixed feelings down the years. 'A galumphing mass', said one; and in 1963 the *Observer's* 'Mammon' column condemned it as 'the most spiritually depressing building in London'. Martin Briggs, however, considered it to be 'a very fine building', but he was looking at it from the river. Two other major buildings were constructed on the fringe of Pimlico in the 1930s. Victoria Coach Station, designed by Wallis Gilbert and Partners, was opened in 1932 to replace a temporary site on Lupus Street that soon became part of the Tachbrook Estate. Pevsner describes it as 'an impressive demonstration of the new architectural style': it has recently been both modernised and restored, and very well too.

Pevsner was less impressed with the 'ghastly piece of oversized sculpture' above the entrance to the new Imperial Airways terminal, which opened in June 1939 just across the road, but at the time this stretch of Buckingham Palace Road must have seemed very modern and progressive. *The Westminster*

and Pimlico News certainly thought so: 'Reaching up into the blue, 175 feet above the coils of mortal man, the huge clock-faced tower in Buckingham Palace Road symbolises the reaching out of this great organisation'. Airways House (now the National Audit Office) adjoins the railway, and Imperial Airways were proud to announce that 'Empire passengers will leave for Southampton by special train from the company's private station in the rear of the premises', where they embarked on a flying boat from Southampton Water. Those with non-Imperial destinations had to content themselves with a coach shuttle to Croydon Aerodrome.

Old Chelsea Bridge was swept away in 1935, a victim of the huge increase in motor traffic, which doubled between 1914 and 1929. By September the piers of the new bridge were already above the waterline, and throughout the length of the temporary wooden bridge built for pedestrians, knots in the planks had been poked out by little (and perhaps by not-so-little) boys anxious for a bird's-eye view of the work going on below. The new bridge

Reaching up into the blue - Airways House.

was opened in 1937 by Mackenzie King, the Prime Minister of Canada, who in his speech afterwards declared that 'in the building of bridges there is a symbolism which represents the cement of the British Empire itself'. The winds of change blew the Empire away, but the bridge remains: by the 1960s it had become London's busiest.

The rise of Hitler, and the prospect of another war, cast a long shadow over 1930s Pimlico as elsewhere. Dolphin Square was, according to the builders, 'built with a war in mind ... constructed of reinforced concrete and designed in such a way that any bomb damage would be minimised'. The British Union of Fascists, who held their meetings in the King's Road, were busy in Pimlico. As early as 1928, the Mayor of Westminster paid tribute to 'the work of the Church Army, Salvation Army, Boy Scouts, Fascisti and others' in supporting victims of the flood disaster, and in 1935 a woman from Vauxhall Bridge Road was bound over for chalking the words 'Fascism next time' on a Millbank wall. She claimed to have been pestered by Jews 'because I smashed up their meeting in Hyde Park one Sunday'.

William Joyce, the sinister 'Lord Haw Haw' of Hitler's radio propaganda service, had an office in Vauxhall Bridge Road before the war. He used to preach to the locals in Tachbrook Street Market on the decadent state of England and its rulers; but in fact the sympathies of the authorities at this time were often with the fascists. 'It is a great mistake to attempt to introduce anything political into a purely sporting and social event', a magistrate told the defendants as he sentenced them to the maximum fine of £2 each for handing out anti-Nazi leaflets to German football fans at Victoria in 1935. Two months earlier, fascists were fined five shillings for flyposting, and told to 'go away, don't do it again' - because, as the magistrate said, 'they meant well, these young Fascists, their intention being to avert needless war'.

Chelsea Bridge under construction.

69

8 Pimlico at War

Cumberland Street after the doodlebug.

'It was just as though a huge orange flare had gone up under your feet. A hell of a bang .... then dead, dead silence. Then, as though some time afterwards, a slow shower of bricks from everywhere'. These were the words of a stretcher-bearer, rescuing people from the debris of Sutherland Terrace on the night of 16 April 1941, known to Pimlico people thereafter as 'The Wednesday' because of the devastation it caused. Three high explosive bombs and a parachute mine destroyed the whole street, including Pimlico's oldest pub, the famous Monster. A large slice of Ebury Street and a factory in Grosvenor Road were destroyed in the same raid, and a mine landed in Lillington Street, killing forty people.

The 'Phoney War' had, for Pimlico, been a period of great activity. Many of Pimlico's 36,000 people were evacuated, and 8,000 of Cubitt's sturdily-built coal-cellars were converted by the Council into shelters. Steel bunks were installed and electricity was laid on. Some of them were quite snug; one shelter featured 'walls washed pink, the electric light shaded and a well-protected landlady surrounded by her brood of lodgers'. Pimlico's war began in earnest in the late summer of 1940. A delayed-action bomb that September cleared the site (now a playground) in Sussex Street, and two hundred people lost their homes. A parachute mine the following month fell in Cambridge Street where Russell House now stands, killing twenty-three people and leaving 300 homeless in three-quarters of an acre of rubble. Just before Christmas a huge explosion - one of London's largest - on the railway line by Ebury Bridge shattered glass in Knightsbridge and rained chunks of railway all over Pimlico. A four-foot slice of sleeper was found next to Dolphin Square. Things quietened down considerably after that terrible winter, but Pimlico was once more a major target in 1944, when the 'doodlebug' attacks began.

Public shelter in a pavement vault.

One of the first flying bombs cleared the site of the present Catholic Church in Winchester Street, killing thirteen and wounding 150, and there were more devastating raids that summer on Peabody Avenue and Westmoreland Terrace.

Morale, on the whole, was nonetheless high throughout the war. One old lady, a victim of the Ebury Bridge blast, was found stoically stirring her stew in the ruins of her kitchen: another was spotted emptying her rubbish in the crater where her dustbin had always stood. Six months before 'The Wednesday', the landlord of the doomed Monster launched a 'Buy a Spitfire' appeal with a record that began 'Achtung, Achtung!' and ended with the memorable line 'Fourpence a day keeps the bombers away'. The railings of the squares were melted down for the war effort, and some of the squares themselves were converted into allotments: market gardening thus briefly returned to what had once been the old Neat House Gardens.

Pimlico's war damage was considerable. Four hundred houses were destroyed or had to be demolished; every street bore its toll. Barely a house escaped without some damage. Some of the bomb sites still remain, empty reminders of the devastation; but to me as a child, Pimlico's most potent war souvenirs were the stencilled notices, still to be seen on some street corners, announcing the 'Public Shelters in Vaults under Pavements in this Street'.

The first anti-gas test took place at Pimlico, on 29 March 1941. Instructing people where to go.

Queen Elizabeth, wife of George VI, visits the Air Raid Warden's post in the basement of 33 Warwick Square.

9 A Good Humanity

Despite the promise of the poster, 'Passport to Pimlico' featured little in the way of 'French goings-on' - and nothing at all of Pimlico.

Plan for Pimlico

People who lived through the War often say that it brought them together as never before. True or otherwise, Pimlico in 1949 suddenly became a by-word across the world for a close-knit urban community, self-contained, slightly run-down, eccentric and supportive. Passport to Pimlico was released that spring; and in this famous Ealing Comedy, a place called Pimlico secedes from the United Kingdom after London's last unexploded bomb goes off. 'The essence of the film is English good humour', said the Times review, but it is a shame that the film itself was filmed somewhere else entirely, as Jane Hylton, who starred in it, was no doubt told many times when she came to Pimlico SW1 that summer to open the St Gabriel's Summer Fete. For at that time the real Pimlico would have fitted the bill quite nicely.

'Though much of the facade may be poor, there is in Pimlico a good humanity abroad', wrote William Sansom in 1947. 'There is the impression that here not a few families but many people live ... at first sight bleak: but here people live, it is a place of residence if it is not grand; and if the soot clings too easily and if the railway does run too near the backyard - then there are compensations, for the pram's out in the alley and the washing's on the line, the steps scrubbed and the house in order, there's a square round the corner with trees in it, a pub with beer in it and a lively line of barrows lending an affection to the upper end of Lupus Street'.

Pimlico had need of its 'good humanity' after the war, for the place was a mess. 'On the whole, Pimlico was well planned and served its purpose for a century, but was already becoming shabby when the Second World War led to great damage by bombing,' wrote Martin Briggs in 1949. 'Nowadays, much of it is derelict and ripe for rebuilding'. Briggs was maybe unaware that the City Council had plans to do just that. In 1944, they produced a 'Plan for Pimlico', drawn up by two of the foremost planners of the day. 'The general appearance of Pimlico is drab', they declared, and proposed to flatten it and start again. A third of Cubitt's Pimlico was laid out in roads - 'an unduly large proportion', it was felt. 'A large number of streets can be considered as redundant or uneconomic', so most of them were to go. Gloucester Street was to become a major route, extended to Vauxhall Bridge Road in one direction and the river in the other. Grosvenor Road and Vauxhall Bridge Road were to be widened to a width of a hundred feet or more.

Pimlico's existing shopping area totalled twelve acres, which was considered to be 'excessive'. The plan proposed to halve it, and concentrate facilities in two 'local shopping zones' on Lupus Street and 'on the site now occupied by Alderney and Winchester Streets which is absorbed into a residential unit in our proposals'. Acknowledging that Pimlico 'has always been regarded as the most extensive dormitory of Westminster', the Council thought that it would be possible to house Pimlico's proposed population of 30,000 in blocks of flats five to ten storeys high. The lower blocks were to be at the north-west end, around Warwick Way; eight-storey blocks were to flank the western fringes, with the tallest blocks along Vaux-

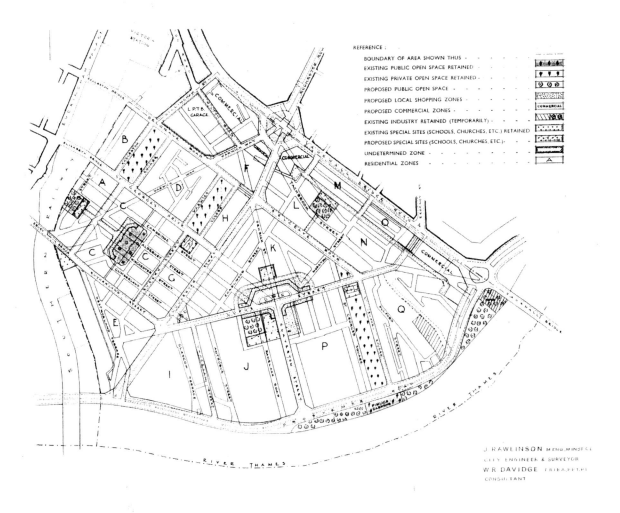

How Pimlico might have been: the 'Plan for Pimlico', 1946.

hall Bridge Road and the river. In the end - mercifully, most would say - a much more modest rebuilding programme was introduced. To this we owe Russell House in Cambridge Street, the flats in Ebury Square, and the first phase of the Abbots Manor

estate in Warwick Way, opened in 1955; built on the site of the abbot of Westminster's house, the blocks were named after famous abbeys.

This Jewel by the River

The biggest scheme by far was the famous Churchill Gardens estate, between Lupus Street and the river. Land had been offered cheaply to the Council here as long ago as 1924, and in 1936 the Council believed it to be 'the cheapest site available anywhere in the city which would justify its acquisition for a housing scheme for the working classes', but little had been done by the time that war broke out. After the War, a thirty-two acre site was cleared, consisting, it was said, of 'old houses in a dreary maze of narrow streets with mixed industrial development'.

Abbots Manor: Sherbourne House in the foreground, Glastonbury Tower (1972) behind. The Neat House once stood on this corner.

The site of Churchill Gardens. Dolphin Square is in the background.

Churchill Gardens.

Three docks, including Bramah's and Octavius Smith's (still known locally as 'Distillery Dock') were also filled in. An architectural competition was held in 1946, with a brief to house some 1,600 families on the site. High density and the need for open space meant that the buildings had to be quite tall, but the winning firm of Powell and Moya fulfilled their brief with such a light hand that their huge development complements Cubitt's Pimlico instead of dwarfing it.

The estate was named Churchill Gardens, after a well-known former resident of Pimlico, and the facilities were unusually good. They included hot water on tap - piped across the river from Battersea Power Station, where it had been used for cooling, and stored in a 130-foot high accumulator, dubbed the 'Pimlico Polygon'. Churchill Gardens was a great success with its tenants, a third of whom had moved there from inadequate and overcrowded places in Pimlico and elsewhere in the city. In 1964, well over half the residents described the estate as 'a friendly place to live in'. 'After fourteen years in hell in the West End', said one housewife, 'this is paradise'. The critics loved it too. 'This jewel by the river', said one. It gave one 'new grounds for believing in the future of London', said the *New Statesman*. 'An obsolete quarter of old London is being erased and a piece of a completely new London is being built'. 'If you go to see this building', said another, 'go again at night when the lights are on the staircases and on the balconies, and you will see that a great modern building can take on an air of romance as well as the most Gothick of them'.

The last blocks of flats were finally completed in 1962, but to some the Churchill Gardens estate was not completed until Pimlico School was opened in 1970, on land that had been ear-marked since the fifties. It

The western end of Warwick Way shortly before demolition.

was built for 1,725 pupils, which was considerably more than the recommended number for the four-and-a-half acre site, so the architects tried to make the building as light as possible by using a vast amount of glass in its construction. Pevsner in 1973 considered it to be 'the weirdest recent building in London ... restless, aggressive, exciting'. Time's verdict has been harsher: too hot in summer, too cold in winter, and costly to maintain; and as this book goes to press plans are afoot to rebuild it.

A Fashionable Odour of Decay

The impact of Churchill Gardens on the rest of Pimlico was tremendous, not least because it attracted so much outside interest to the area. The estate won many architectural awards, and a great deal of international acclaim, which did much to stimulate the renovation of Pimlico's run-down hinterland. The Centre for Urban Studies contrasted the bright new blocks of Churchill

Gardens - 'glittering by night, assertive by day' - with the 'streets of decaying terrace houses' on the other side of Lupus Street. 'Far from depressing property values in the district, the very existence of the estate ... has undoubtedly stimulated private development'.

'I like Pimlico immensely. It has a lot of character', declared a Moreton Street resident in 1961, and it was the character of Pimlico, its somewhat run-down charm, that began to attract discerning residents back into Mr Cubitt's District. William Sansom, who wrote in 1947, was clearly taken with the place, despite 'much sooted London brick, much grey and falling plaster', and though the character in Gavin Douglas' novel was told that Cubitt's houses were 'a bastardised Georgian smothered in Victorian ornamentation', his first impression 'of both buildings and roadway was pleasant, for I liked the width of the roadway and the green trees and grass of the several squares among the buildings'.

During the 1950s, unfashionable central areas such as Pimlico began to attract the attention of a new generation of young professional types, to whom suburbia had no appeal. My father, who moved to a St George's Square flat in 1956, and is still in Pimlico forty years later, recalls the surprise he felt at finding this 'socially mixed and distinctly pleasant residential area, amazingly central, which hadn't been spoilt'. First to be renovated were the squares, where pioneers such as Victor Valentine began to buy up the head-leases of houses which had been requisitioned during the war, and converted the large, dilapidated houses into high-quality flats.

In 1950, the Grosvenor Estate sold off much of its property in Pimlico, which swelled the number of available houses considerably. Equally significant was the insistence of firms such as Royd's, who were selling eighty-year leases on houses north of Warwick Way and west of Sutherland Street, that purchasers were to renovate their properties and not to sub-let them. Royd's agents Roy Brooks helped to put Pimlico on the map of every house-buyer in London with a series of candid and witty advertisements that became compulsory reading for many: 'There is a fashionable odour of decay in this Pimlico residence. 8/9 rooms in a horrible state of decoration, innocent of all modern amenities. Mini-mud patch at rear. Single family occupancy only as sub-letting not allowed in this fashionable slum development'.

The 'gentrification' of Pimlico was under way, but it brought a great deal of hardship to many people in its wake. Amongst its first and most surprising victims were the 1,200 tenants of Dolphin Square, which was sold in 1959 to a speculator. A tenants' association appeared, and eventually managed to convince the City Council to buy the whole estate on their behalf: the Dolphin Square Trust was set up to run it. There was, not surprisingly, some criticism; but, as the Secretary said in 1962, 'contrary to popular belief most tenants here are ordinary middle-class people, and many of the flats are not as nice as those put up by the Council in Churchill Gardens opposite'.

Pimlico's rising prestige meant that rents began to increase sharply. As early as 1961 there were complaints that Pimlico houses were being 'tarted up' as a prelude to massive rent increases. 'I know of one woman in Pimlico who seems to specialise in this kind of thing,' an LCC councillor stormed. 'As soon as she can acquire a house she does it up and then lets it at a high rent'. Houses were being left empty by landlords holding out for twelve pounds a week; evictions were becoming commonplace.

Dolphin Square.

A Very Human Environment

Not everyone saw the potential for 'tarting up' Cubitt's Pimlico. The district once more narrowly escaped wholesale redevelopment

Lillington Street in 1963.

in 1961, when an American corporation's plans to build 'a whole group of high-rise structures' on a 24-acre site were refused. The City Council itself still believed that large-scale redevelopment was necessary, because of the chronic shortage of building land in Westminster and the persistent problem of overcrowding, and proposed to demolish some fifteen acres between Tachbrook Street and Vauxhall Bridge Road.

The Council justified its choice of site by pointing out that the houses were in poor condition. Half of them had no bathrooms, and in many cases several families had to share a WC. The plan was hotly and skilfully contested, however, by many of the 842 families who lived there. The residents agreed that the houses 'had begun to look shabby, and were a blot on the landscape of Pimlico', but pointed out that the threat of demolition which had hung over the area since the war had not inspired home-owners to brighten

the place up. They suggested that renovation would be just as effective and quite possibly cheaper - 'if [the houses] had been sited in Chelsea, they would have been restored and sold at a considerable profit', said one - but restoration was not yet in vogue, and the scheme went ahead.

As with Churchill Gardens, architects were invited to compete for the design; the judge was Philip Powell, of Powell & Moya, and Churchill Gardens fame. Lillington Gardens was the result: very different to Churchill Gardens, but just as successful. Architects Darbourne & Darke combined the same requirement for high density with a feeling for the small scale of old urban communities: Powell described their design as 'a renewal of the existing urban pattern - a break with its drabness, but not with its scale'. A high proportion of flats were therefore designed with direct access to street-level, while every

Lillington Gardens.

house has its own garden. The result, as a government minister said, is 'a very human environment' - intimate, homely and interesting.

The Tube of Happiness

Pimlico's tube station was something of an afterthought. The Brixton extension of the Victoria line received official blessing in August 1967, but London Transport repeatedly maintained that a station at Pimlico would not pay its way. Local support was fulsome and wholehearted: the case for a station was 'absolutely unassailable and completely urgent', as one councillor put it, but work only began on the new station once the government had agreed to contribute to the cost of building it.

The engineers' task was not easy: the river Tyburn runs underground within a few yards of the booking-hall, and the riverside topsoil was so loose that the ground had to be artificially frozen for the shaft to be sunk. And there was worse, for in 1969 the miners encountered 'a large black presence' in the southbound running tunnel. It was said 'to have induced considerable fear in those who have seen it'. The favoured theory was that the line there passed beneath a plague-pit, the 'presence' some hideous emanation from

its victims, but it might have been just some Will-o'the-wisp, lingering from the days when Pimlico was a marsh, who will maybe yet emerge from the elegantly-disguised air-vent in Moreton Street to surprise a passer-by.

The station was structurally complete, and the platforms finished, by July 1971 when Princess Alexandra formally opened the Brixton extension by travelling from Pimlico. It was another fourteen months before the station was opened to the public. The Lord Mayor of Westminster did the honours. He hoped that the station 'would give happiness to all using it', an intriguing sentiment. Curious passengers, happy or otherwise, were at last able to study at close quarters the rectangle of yellow dots that make up the station's bizarre motif; its purpose is to remind travellers that even stranger works of art are to be seen in the Tate Gallery, just around the corner. The new station, indeed, was nearly named after the famous gallery, but local opinion luckily won the day.

Heartbreak Homes

The City Council was understandably proud of its record in having 'carried out and encouraged extensive redevelopment and improvement of houses'; but to some they rather spoilt it by sanctioning the construction of Glastonbury House, the district's only skyscraper, which was opened in 1972. Next year, the rest of Cubitt's Pimlico was designated as a Conservation Area, and the threat of wholesale demolition disappeared.

Elsewhere in Pimlico, the process of gentrification continued at a fairly sedate pace throughout the sixties. The sea of newly-painted stucco spread slowly southwards, reaching Clarendon Street, it seemed to this small boy, around 1970. Property prices now began to go sky-high: in one year, 1972, the price of a typical four-storey house doubled. The sharks began to home in on the four-fifths of Pimlico people who still lived in privately-rented dwellings. Unscrupulous

  Evening News

A SPECIAL EVENING NEWS SERIES

What the property developer is doing to Pimlico

THE SERIES ALL LONDON IS TALKING ABOUT—See Page Ten

PRESSURE ON TENANTS: MP SEEKS ACTION

When life began to turn sour in Pimlico

Steel sacking
Michael Foo
steps into r

St George's Estate i

caught in the noose

Now more
MPs seek
Pimlico
inquiry

GONE—
the house
of her dreams

HOUSEWIVES
TO PICKET
SHOPS IN
PRICES
REVOLT

developers began to empty their properties: in just eighteen months, it was said that over 2,000 tenants had been given notice to quit. Pimlico became notorious. Several reports, and a series of *Evening News* feature articles on Pimlico's 'Heartbreak Homes', led local MPs to ask the Government for 'remedial measures', and the City Council embarked upon a policy of purchasing houses for the benefit of less affluent locals. Policies such as these have ensured that less well-off people are still able to live within Cubitt's Pimlico, which, by central London standards, still has an unusually good social mix.

Postscript

Pimlico today is a place of gleaming stucco, ruched curtains and sleek, expensive cars. The corner shops now sell antiques, and the only litter on the streets is the litter bins themselves, on every corner. Pimlico is a place where the wealthy choose to live: South Belgravia has arrived at last. Thomas Cubitt would be delighted.

Winchester Street interior after conversion, 1973.

List of Sources

Readers who would like to find out more about Pimlico may find much of interest in two excellent recent publications - Isobel Watson's *Westminster and Pimlico Past* (1993), and Roy Harrison's *Blitz over Westminster* (1990). K F Morris' *A History of Dolphin Square* (1995), is pretty comprehensive, and tenacious readers may also find useful material in William Carey's *Pimlico* (1986). I have made extensive use throughout of Hermione Hobhouse's magnificent biography *Thomas Cubitt: Master Builder* (1995), especially for chapter 4 (The Building of Pimlico). Other principal sources are listed below.

I have consulted a fair number of original documents, mostly relating to the activities of the Grosvenor Estate and the various local authorities responsible for Pimlico, from the sixteenth century to the present. For those inspired to dig deeper, most of the sources I have used can be found at the City of Westminster Archives Centre, where there is potential for further research among their extensive holdings. There I have deposited a more detailed list of the sources I have used, chapter by chapter, for those who want to check the evidence for themselves.

Books

Aldis, C R *Lecture on the Sanitary Conditions of Large Towns and of Belgravia*, 1857

Battersea Park and Embankment Act, 1846

Bennett, F *The Story of W J E Bennett*, 1909

Blunt, R *The Wonderful Village*, 1918

Bolton, F J *London's Water Supply*, 1884

Booth, C *Life and Labour of the People of London*, 3rd series 'Religious Influences', vol 3, 1902

Briggs, M S *Down the Thames*, 1949

Bullen, A H (ed) 'Pimlyco, or, Runne Red-cap'(1609), in *Ancient Drolleries*, no 2, 1891

Carter, K *London and the Famous*, 1982

Chambers, R *Book of Days*, vol 2, 1863-4

Chelsea Waterworks Act, 1852

City of Westminster, *City of Westminster Plan*, 1946

City of Westminster, *Official Guide*, 1934

City of Westminster, *Plan for Pimlico*, 1946

City of Westminster, *Report of the Medical Officer of Health*, 1935

Clinch, G *Mayfair and Belgravia: being an Historical Account of the Parish of St George Hanover Square*, 1892

Davis, R G *Memorials of the Hamlet of Knightsbridge*, 1859

Day, J R *The Story of London's Underground*, 1979

Day, J R *The Story of the Victoria Line*, 1969

Day, J R *The Brixton Extension of the Victoria Line*, 1971

Denney, M *London's Waterways*, 1977

Dickinson, H W *Water Supply of London*, 1953

Douglas, G *A Tale of Pimlico*, 1948

Edmonds, R *Chelsea, from the Five Fields to the Worlds End*, 1956

Emerson, G *London: How the Great City Grew*, 1862

Gatty, C T *Mary Davies and the Manor of Ebury*, 1921

Glass, R (ed) *London: Aspects of Change*, 1964

Gomme, G L *London 1837-97*, 1898

Harvey, B *Westminster Abbey and its Estates in the Middle Ages*, 1977

Herbert, A P *Dolphin Square*, 1935

Holmes, T *Chelsea*, 1972

Howard, P *London's River*, 1975

Johnston's London Directory, 1817

Keppel, G T *Fifty Years of My Life*, vol 1, 1876

Lancaster, M J *Brian Howard*, 1968

London County Council, Public Control Department, *London's Markets*, 1893

London School of Economics, *New Survey of London Life and Labour*, 1928, vol 6, 1934

MacNeil, I *Joseph Bramah: a Century of Invention*, 1968

McMaster, J *A Short History of St Martin's in the Fields*, 1916

Metcalf, P *The Park Town Estate and the Battersea Tangle*, 1978

Metcalf, P *Victorian London*, 1972

Metropolitan Improvements, second report, 1845

Metropolitan Water Board, *Water Supply of London*, 1961

Middleton, J *View of the Agriculture of Middlesex*, 1798

Nightingale, Revd *Beauties of England and Wales*, vol 3, 1816

Pearson, P *Pimlico: Crisis for Furnished Tenants*, [c1973]

Pevsner, N *Buildings of England*, vol 1, 3rd ed, 1973

Phillips, Sir R *A Morning's Walk from London to Kew*, 1820

Pimlico Neighbourhood Aid Centre, *Planning Policy and Evictions in Pimlico*, 1974

Report on the River Thames, 1858

Richmond, L and Turton, A *The Brewing Industry: a Guide to Historical Records*, 1990

Rosa, J G *Colonel Colt, London*, 1976

St Gabriel's Parish Year Books, 1892, 1900.

Sansom, W *Westminster in War*, 1947

Sheppard, F *London 1808-70: The Infernal Wen*, 1971

Shirley, T F *The First Hundred Years: The Story of St Gabriel's, Pimlico 1853-1953*, 1953

Smith, J E *St John the Evangelist: Parochial Memoirs*, 1892

Sullivan, D *The Westminster Corridor*, 1994

Tanner, L E *The History of the Coronation*, 1952

Tarn, J N *Five Per Cent Philanthropy*, 1973

The Thames, *Waterway of the World*, 1893

Timb, *Curiosities of London*, 1871

Trollope, A *The Small House at Allington*, vol 2, 1864

Victoria Station and Pimlico Railway Act, 1858

Walford, E *Old and New London*, vol 5, 1897

Westminster Housing Trust, *The Tachbrook Estate*, 1949

Woodworth, F *Victoria Coach Station: the First Fifty Years 1932-1981*, 1982

Woolmer, E *All Around Pimlico*, 1922

Wroth, W W *The London Pleasure-Gardens of the Eighteenth Century*, 1896

Periodical Articles

Chick, A 'Matthias Koops in London', *Antiquarian Books Monthly Review*, April 1985

Draper, E 'Reminiscences of Westminster', *Westminster*, June 1897

Notes and Queries, vol 1, 1850, 1852; 3rd series, vol 4, 1863; 4th series, vol 8, 1877; 7th series, vol 12, 1891; 10th series, vol 10-11, 1908-9

Rosenfeld, S 'Two Westminster Theatres', *Theatre Notebook* [n.d.]

Rutton, W L 'The Manor of Eia', *Archaeologia*, vol LXII, 1910

'St Michael's School', *Evangelical Magazine*, October 1848

Theses and Other Unpublished Work

'Dolphin and Grand Junction Nuisance', 1827; Hazelton-Swayles, M J 'Urban Aristocrats: the Grosvenors and the Development of Belgravia and Pimlico in the Nineteenth Century', unpub PhD thesis, Bedford College, 1981; copies of both are to be found at the City of Westminster Archives Centre.

Scrapbooks and Cuttings

Foster, D (compiler) 'Inns, taverns, alehouses, coffee houses etc in and around London', 82 vols of scrapbooks; held at City of Westminster Archives Centre.

'Papers Relating to Pimlico, 1839-85'; held at British Library.

Index

Cundy, Thomas	46	Garden Row	28, 54
Dangerfield, Miss	36	Gardeners	11, 28, 29, 30
Darbourne and Darke	79	Gardens	
David Copperfield	23	see *Neat House Gardens*	
Davies, Alexander	27	Gaspey, William	54
Davies, Mary	27	George II	18
Davis, Baby Vi	61	George III	18
Davis, R G	5	George IV	25, 26
Defoe, Daniel	17	Ghosts	80
Denbigh Street	35, 67	Glamorgan Street	63
Dickens, Charles	23, 27, 44	Glasgow Terrace	53
Diorama	43	Glastonbury House	80
Distillery Dock	76	Glastonbury Tower	75
Distillery Lane	35, 53	Gloucester Street	61, 74
Docks	23, 28, 33, 76	Gourdemaine, Margerie	9
Dog fighting	20	Grand Junction Waterworks	39
Dolphin Square	35, 67, 68, 69, 70, 75, 78	Grant, Washington	61
Doodlebugs	70, 71	Great Western Railway	55, 56
Douglas, Gavin	66, 77	Greene, William	13
Dove's	61	Grosvenor, Sir Thomas	27
Dwarf, The	18	Grosvenor Basin, The	31
Eaton Square	46	Grosvenor Canal	12, 15, 28, 31, 32, 33, 36, 40, 53, 54, 55, 65
Ebury, Manor of	7, 9, 10, 27	Grosvenor Estate	12, 23, 24, 27, 28, 2 9, 30, 33, 35, 36, 40, 46, 56, 57, 59, 61, 78
Ebury Bridge	8, 15, 35, 54, 56, 70, 71		
Ebury Bridge Estate	65		
Ebury Bridge Road	31		
Ebury House	8	Grosvenor Hotel	23, 56, 65
Ebury Square	18, 75	Grosvenor Place	20
Ebury Street	12, 20, 44, 70	Grosvenor Road	7, 29, 38, 39, 46, 64, 65, 70, 74
Eccleston Bridge	12, 32, 35		
Eccleston Square	33, 34, 37, 45, 46, 54	Guildhouse	65
Eccleston Square Chapel	46, 65	Gwyn, Helena	17
Eccleston Street	35, 39	Gwyn, John	27, 29
Edward II	9	Gwyn, Nell	17
Eia, Manor of see *Ebury*		Hamilton House Hotel	25
Elephant, The	13	Hammond, Revd James	55
Elizabeth, Queen Mother	72	Hands, Mrs	18
Elizabeth Street	35	Health	7, 39, 40, 41
Elliott's Brewhouse see *Stag Brewery*		Heartbreak Homes	81, 82
Embankment	38, 64	Heberfield, William	25
Entertainment see *Leisure*		Hengier, Signora	21
Equitable Gasworks	54	Henry VIII	10
Fabricotti's	45	Herbert, A P	67
Fascists	69	Highwaymen	5, 20
Fellowship Guild	65	Holbein Place	5
Fireworks	17, 21	Holy Trinity Church	46
Five Fields	5	Hooper, Dr	39
Five Fields Row	20	Horseferry Road	56
Floods	34, 63, 64, 65	Horwood's map, 1795	5
Food	10, 11, 14, 18	Housing	12, 27, 28, 32, 33, 36, 37, 38, 54, 59, 60, 63, 65, 66, 67, 74, 75, 76, 77, 78, 79, 80, 81, 82
Franke, William	38		
Fun, The	13		